Bringing ABA to
Home, School, and Play
for Young Children with
Autism Spectrum Disorders
and Other Disabilities

Bringing ABA to Home, School, and Play for Young Children with Autism Spectrum Disorders and Other Disabilities

by

Debra Leach, Ed.D., BCBA
Winthrop University
Department of Counseling, Leadership, and Educational Studies
Rock Hill, South Carolina

·P A U L·H·
BROOKES
PUBLISHING CO ®

Baltimore • London • Sydney

Paul H. Brookes Publishing Co.
Post Office Box 10624
Baltimore, Maryland 21285-0624
USA

www.brookespublishing.com

Cover photo: © Mike Martin
Typeset by Integrated Publishing Solutions, Grand Rapids, Michigan.
Manufactured in the United States of America by
Sheridan Books, Inc., Chelsea, Michigan.

Table 2.1 and Figures 3.1, 3.2, 3.3, 3.4, 3.5, 6.1, 6.3, 6.4, and 6.5 are from Leach, D. (2010). *Bringing ABA into your inclusive classroom: A guide to improving outcomes for students with autism spectrum disorders.* Baltimore: Paul H. Brookes Publishing Co., Inc.; adapted by permission.

Library of Congress Cataloging-in-Publication Data

Leach, Debra.
    Bringing ABA to home, school, and play for young children with autism spectrum disorders and other disabilities / by Debra Leach.
        p.   cm.
    Includes bibliographical references and index.
    ISBN-13: 978-1-59857-240-7
    ISBN-10: 1-59857-240-7
1. Autistic children—Education.   2. Autistic children—Behavior modification.   3. Behavior therapy for children.   I. Title.

    LC4718.L44 2012
    371.94—dc23   2012021089

British Library Cataloguing in Publication data are available from the British Library.

2016   2015   2014   2013   2012

10   9   8   7   6   5   4   3   2   1

Contents

· ·

About the Author

Debra Leach, Ed.D., BCBA, is Assistant Professor of Special Education at Winthrop University and a Board Certified Behavior Analyst. She previously served as a public school teacher, as an early intervention provider, and as Associate Director for the Florida Atlantic University Center for Autism and Related Disabilities. Her main research interests include autism spectrum disorders, inclusion, applied behavior analysis, positive behavior supports, and early intervention. She enjoys training preservice teachers and working with school districts, families, and community groups to support the successful inclusion of children, adolescents, and adults with autism spectrum disorders in home, school, and community contexts.

Foreword

The number of children receiving autism services in inclusive educational settings has greatly increased over the past two decades, but there has not been a corresponding growth in teacher training to address those increasing educational needs. Misconceptions concerning the nature of autism and limited understanding of instructional strategies applicable to this special education population creates challenges for integrated educational services for students with autism (National Council for the Accreditation of Teacher Education, 2010; Williams, Schroeder, Carvalho, & Cervantes, 2011).

The present book addresses some of these needs, presenting an introduction to applied behavior analysis (ABA) methods for children with autism in inclusive school settings. Not only does it address the legal mandate of natural environment intervention (IDEA, 2004), it makes a persuasive case for the educational and social value of the approach for children with autism. While there are differences in emphasis among behavioral education practitioners working with young children with autism, the general principles underlying the various methods are shared in common across the field. However, these approaches differ somewhat along several dimensions in the specific ways those principles are applied in day to day practice (Thompson, 2011):

Natural	Structured
Group	Individual
Distributed across time	Intensive
Child directed	Adult directed
Natural cues and consequences	Engineered cues and consequences
Loosely structured (incidental)	Highly structured (discrete trial)
Task based	Routines/activities based
Integrated	Categorically delivered

Many of the early developers of applied behavioral interventions with children with autism had success using approaches nearer the *functional* end of these continua, and as a result were convinced those were the most effective and appropriate (Maurice, 1994). They have tended to argue in favor of intensive discrete trial intervention up to 30 hours per week, often in home settings but sometimes in schools as well (Leaf & McEachin, 1999). Over the intervening years, researchers and practitioners have employed methods similar to those toward the more *naturalistic* end of each of these continua with equally favorable results with some children (Koegel, Koegel, Harrower, & Carter, 1999). In reality, there are limited data from well-controlled studies with matched students with autism that provide clear evidence for the precise points along these dimensions that are most appropriate *for a given child.*

Nonetheless, it is broadly clear, many students with moderate to mild autism symptoms and limited challenging behavior profit from interventions nearer the naturalistic end of these continua, while other children with no means of communication, who lack social interest and responsiveness, and who exhibit frequent nonfunctional repetitive behavior and other behavioral challenges, tend to make more rapid gains in programs nearer the functional end of these continua. Often, once a child with greater challenges has begun to master basic skills, it is possible to transition to a more naturalistic approach.

In *Individualized Autism Intervention for Young Children: Blending Discrete Trial and Naturalistic Strategies* (Thompson, 2011) there is a scale that can be used to attempt to identify the blend of these dimensions that are most appropriate for each child (AIRS™; Autism Intervention Responsiveness Scale). Research shows that about 25% of preschool children on the autism spectrum function extremely well in totally naturalistic intervention settings, and about half achieve similar gains in a blend of naturalistic with some more structured intervention early in intervention (Thompson et al., in press), while the remainder make modest gains within a more structured approach. The latter children have a good deal in common with students with more significant developmental delays, which may actually represent their major educational challenge.

This book is written clearly with compelling examples drawing upon the author's extensive experience as an early intervention provider working with toddlers with autism and their families, as well as working with classroom teachers. In Chapter 5, Debra Leach does an excellent job of introducing some of the most common behavioral methods for intervening with children with autism.

There is a world of difference between understanding the basic principles and being able to take the necessary practical steps to actually implement behavioral interventions in the classroom. This book provides extensive forms to be completed by classroom teachers that guide the practitioners through the practical steps of applying the basic principles, which can be at times challenging, even to experienced teachers. For years to come, Leach's *Bringing ABA to Home, School, and Play for Young Children with Autism Spectrum Disorders and Other Disabilities* will serve as an effective guide to both special and general education teachers and other school personnel working with students with autism.

Travis Thompson, Ph.D.
Special Education Program
Department of Educational Psychology
University of Minnesota
Minneapolis, MN

REFERENCES

Cooper, J.O., Heron, T.E., & Heward, W.L. (2007). *Applied behavior analysis* (2nd ed.) Upper Saddle River, NJ: Pearson.

Individuals with Disabilities Education Act of 1990, PL 101-476, 20 U.S.C., § 1400 *et seq.*

Individuals with Disabilities Education Improvement Act of 2004, PL 108-446, 20 U.S.C. § 1400 *et seq.*

Koegel, L.K., Koegel, R.L., Harrower, J.K., & Carter, C.M. (1999). Pivotal response intervention I: Overview of approach. *The Journal of the Association for Persons with Severe Handicaps, 24*(3), 174–185.

Leaf, R., & McEachin, J. (1999). *A work in progress: Behavior management strategies and a curriculum for intensive behavioral treatment of autism.* New York, NY: DRL Books.

Lord, C.E., & McGee, J. (2001). *Educating children with autism.* Committee on Educational Interventions for Children with Autism, Division of Behavioral and Social Sciences and Education. National Research Council. Washington DC: National Academies Press.

Lovaas, O.I. (1987, February). Behavioral treatment and normal educational and intellectual functioning in young autistic children. *Journal of Consulting and Clinical Psychology, 55*(1), 3–9.

Maurice, C. (1994). *Let me hear your voice: A family's triumph over autism.* New York, NY: Ballantine Books.

National Council for the Accreditation of Teacher Education. (2010, November). *Transforming teacher education through clinical practice: A national strategy to prepare effective teachers.* Report of the blue ribbon panel on clinical preparation and partnerships for Improved Student Learning. Washington, DC.

Thompson, T. (2011). *Individualized autism intervention for young children: Blending discrete trial and naturalistic strategies.* Baltimore, MD: Paul H. Brookes Publishing Co., Inc.

Thompson, T., Barsness, L., Anderson, C., Bohannan, A., Burggraff, B., & Dropik, P. (In press). Individualized intensive early behavioral intervention for young children with autism: Predictors of type of treatment and outcomes. *Focus on Autism.*

Williams, K.L., Schroeder, J.L., Carvalho, C., & Cervantes, A. (2011). School personnel knowledge of autism: A pilot survey. *The School Psychologist, 65,* 7–9.

Foreword

Debra Leach has provided a long-awaited breath of fresh air to a field that has started to get musty from firmly held myths, strong biases in treatment options, and professional or disability-group entrenchment. If *Bringing ABA to Home, School, and Play for Young Children with Autism Spectrum Disorders and Other Disabilities* serves to clear some cobwebs and get some children and their families the help they should receive in a way that acknowledges they are people first, it will have been worth the time and care that obviously went into writing the book.

Hovering behind the premises and practices described in *Bringing ABA* are three concepts that support the need for this approach. First, children who can benefit from applied behavior analysis (ABA) are more like other children than different from them. Specialization should not require seclusion. Leach has provided compelling arguments for being able to take an evidence-based approach to children and families, rather than making children and families go to self-contained, separate, and secluded sites. Specialists, such as ABA practitioners, often worry about treatment integrity—how well the practices are actually being implemented. This valid concern can lead to an invalid solution, which is to restrict the people who can implement practices. For example, a Board Certified Behavior Analyst (BCBA; i.e., a member of one particular restrictive group) working with young children will be much more effective in working with the child's regular caregivers than directly with the child in a distraction-free setting. Young children naturally learn (i.e., even without planned intervention) to respond to stimuli that naturally occur in their environments, and they often learn their early skills (think of language and motor movements, for example) through repeated interactions with the environment (objects, spaces, people), distributed over time. The good BCBA therefore will capitalize on this method of learning and work with the adults who are teaching the child, whether we like it or not. They will not seclude the child, work with the child in a highly artificial and "unnatural" setting, and then promise to work on generalization to real life. Instead they will program for generalization (Stokes & Baer, 1977).

We should not underestimate the power of the untouched environment to shape behavior. Many advocates will point out that children with autism spectrum disorders (ASD) and other disabilities do not learn well from the untouched environment, which is why we have *special* education and related services. That's true, but it's not true that these children learn *nothing* from the untouched environment. We have all been amazed to see some children who have significant intellectual or behavioral disabilities functioning in everyday routines fairly competently—going to a restaurant with the family, playing outside with other children nearby, going through the mall, and so on. One of the most obvious features of these sights is how their caregivers—often parents—simply expect them to be able to do these things. One might argue that it's a reciprocal process—that the more competent children promote higher expectations in their parents and the parents' high expectations in turn promote more competence. *Bringing ABA* shows how we can take practices to families to support their parenting, grandparenting, teaching (if a teacher), and so on, by tweaking the environment, not radically changing it nor changing it insufficiently with weak interventions.

Treating children more like other children than like a different breed is related to placing value on their childhoods. Natural environment intervention (NEI) as described in this book allows children to continue living their childhoods while getting intervention. When a high value is placed on services as opposed to interventions, their time in normal activities of early childhood might be compromised. In a study over 10 years ago, the most time spent by typically developing children birth to 2 years of age was in sleeping (86 hours and 1 minute), and playing (24:55) (Hofferth & Sandberg, 2000). Children 3–5 years of age spent most of their time sleeping (76:08), then fairly evenly divided among playing (17:26), watching TV (13:49), and school (12:05). Lynch describes how we do not have to rob children with ASD and other significant disabilities of their playtime to provide them with effective interventions.

The second concept I assume is behind *Bringing ABA* is that regular caregivers need support to intervene with children. Caregivers do not necessarily know the effective, evidence-based practices to carry out with the children in their care. To provide this support, we should begin by assessing functional needs in routines, considering the law mandates that interventions be provided within naturally occurring routines whenever possible (Dunst et al., 2001). By asking families and teachers about the child's engagement, independence, and social relationships in home, community, and school routines as well as what everyone else in the home or classroom is doing in those routines, we get a rich and thick enough description to help the family identify what the child is not doing that they would like him or her doing. This kind of functional assessment for developing an intervention plan lends itself to NEI.

We should support caregivers by respecting them enough to focus on evidence-based practices rather than those minimally supported by research. ABA is a whole compendium of evidence-based practices. Perhaps through this book Leach will help professionals and families realize that a behavioral approach can be an efficient, contextually relevant way of addressing attention problems, tactile defensiveness, and hypersensitivity to sounds.

Our support to families by helping them apply ABA in their everyday routines must be matched with a healthy dose of emotional support. This means trying to make behavior plans as feasible as possible for the individual family. The use of good consultation or coaching can ensure the plan is viable. When we hear about the stress some families of children with ASD or other disabilities are under, we need to make sure the stress does not come from services.

Attending to the emotional well-being of the primary caregiver is important. According to family systems theory (Turnbull, Poston, Minnes, & Summers, 2007), the extent to which that person feels satisfied with his or her routines might have an impact on the quantity and quality of intervention the child receives. Emotional support is more likely to come from informal than formal supports, so professionals should help families identify the extended family, friends, neighbors, and community resources (e.g., religious organizations) in their lives and the strength or lack of support from each source.

As for teachers, who are also natural caregivers when children are in classroom programs, an important type of support they should receive is collaborative consultation that provides them with the gift of feedback. Many teachers receive little relevant feedback about their work with children, and when they do, it is not necessarily done well (Casey & McWilliam, 2011). Whether the child's natural caregivers are families or teachers, they need emotional and feed-back support, respectively.

The third concept I see behind NEI is a consultative philosophy and set of practices. Unless professionals adopt children with ASD and other disabilities, they are simply going to have to shift from a direct, hands-on approach to a consultative one, at least for home-based services. This means no more taking toy bags or irrelevant activities into homes, but rather engaging in joint problem solving with the family to build their capacity to be parents and to intervene with *and enjoy* the child between home visits.

For children enrolled in classroom programs, the preparation of the staff to use ABA embedded in routines determines the extent to which outside professionals (i.e., professionals who are not based in the classroom), such as BCBAs, psychologists, speech-language patholo-gists, and occupational therapists need to provide support. Specialized classroom staff, such as an early childhood special education teacher, would typically need less support than regular early childhood teachers. Regardless, outside professionals should not pull the child out of the classroom or even work with him or her at the side of the room; instead, they should collab-oratively consult with the teaching staff to promote teachers' ability to provide interventions to the child during the many hours between the outside professionals' visits to the room. *Bringing ABA* is entirely consistent with this consultative approach.

This small volume by Leach has the potential to pack a big punch. ABA has been mis-understood because of poor implementation in early childhood, such as practitioners "doing ABA" with children in secluded contexts (e.g., in a room at home while the parent is elsewhere in the house; outside the classroom). To make matters worse, families and professionals have assumed these practices are relevant and effective. But they have not seen how truly powerful they could be if done in a contextually relevant, consultative manner such as described in this book.

R.A. McWilliam, Ph.D.
Director, Center for Child and Family Research
Siskin Children's Institute
Chattanooga, Tennessee

REFERENCES

Casey, A.M., & McWilliam, R.A. (2011). The impact of checklist-based feedback on teachers' use of the zone defense schedule. *Journal of Applied Behavior Analysis, 44,* 397–401.

Dunst, C.J., Bruder, M.B., Trivette, C.M., Hamby, D., Raab, M., & McLean, M. (2001). Characteristics and consequences of everyday natural learning opportunities. *Topics in Early Childhood Special Educa-tion, 21,* 68.

Hofferth, S.L., & Sandberg, J.F. (2000). *How American children spend their time.* Ann Arbor, MI: Univer-sity of Michigan, Population Studies Center at the Institute for Social Research.

Stokes, T.F., & Baer, D.M. (1977). An implicit technology of generalization. *Journal of Applied Behavior Analysis, 10,* 349–367.

Turnbull, A.P., Poston, D.J., Minnes, P., & Summers, J.A. (2007). Providing supports and services that enhance a family's quality of life. In I. Brown, & M. Percy (Eds.), *A comprehensive guide to intellectual and developmental disabilities* (pp. 561–571). Baltimore, MD: Paul H. Brookes Publishing Co., Inc.

Preface

It is well documented that intensive early intervention is essential for young children with autism spectrum disorders (ASD), but how to actually deliver intervention is often debated. Since the late 1980s there has been research support for providing early intensive behavioral intervention (EIBI) using applied behavior analysis (ABA), which traditionally is implemented in one-to-one settings using a teacher-directed approach. Over the past 2 decades, there has been a shift toward using more naturalized behavioral and developmental approaches that emphasize child- and family-centered practices, with intensive interventions embedded within home, school, and community routines rather than segregated settings. Researchers and practitioners are now finding ways to utilize evidence-based ABA approaches without losing the contextual basis of naturally occurring daily routines that provide multiple learning opportunities, enhance child motivation, and promote the generalization of learned skills.

The purpose of this book is to provide practitioners with a framework they can use to guide their everyday work with children and families—a step-by-step process for implementing intensive early intervention within the context of everyday routines using ABA for young children with ASD and related disorders. Chapter 1 provides an overview of the legal mandates for this natural environment intervention (NEI) as well as the research support for planning and delivering early intervention services within the context of everyday home, school, and community routines to enhance child development and to improve the competence and confidence of caregivers in meeting the needs of their children. The chapter also provides an overview of ASD and a discussion of the importance of providing specialized NEI for young children with ASD by systematically embedding ABA interventions within everyday contexts. Chapter 2 provides a brief overview of ABA and describes how it can be applied for young children with ASD and related disabilities in the natural environment. Chapters 3–7 provide tools and procedures needed by early intervention providers for conducting quality assessments, developing meaningful goals, planning interventions, monitoring progress, and fostering collaboration among caregivers and professionals to effectively bring ABA into the everyday routines of young children with ASD and related disabilities.

The practice of embedding ABA within the context of NEI is still in its infancy, and I must admit that when I was first introduced to this idea, I was not completely on board. After so many years of providing one-to-one ABA therapy outside of the everyday routines of children and families, it was hard for me to envision any other way of service delivery. But I asked myself, "What would I do if I had a child with ASD?" The answer was not having a variety of individuals coming into my home to implement an ABA program with my child for 20–40 hours each week. The answer was that I would embed ABA interventions during my everyday interactions with my child throughout the day and train other family members to do the same to provide the level of intensive interventions needed. This was my answer because of the education, training, and experience I have acquired, but the families I work with do not have the same background. To help families learn how to effectively and meaningfully meet the needs of their children in this manner, my role as a direct service provider had to shift to that of a model, coach, and facilitator.

Some may argue that certain young children with ASD need some direct one-to-one ABA interventions outside the context of everyday early childhood routines to develop the basic social interaction skills, communication skills, attending skills, and positive behaviors needed to be able to fully benefit from NEI with embedded ABA interventions. This may, in fact, be true. However, it should not be a one or the other approach. Whether or not supplemental supports and services are needed should not determine whether ABA interventions are embedded in the natural environment for young children with ASD and related disabilities. Every child participates in a variety of naturally occurring routines throughout the day. These routines provide authentic learning opportunities that cannot be replicated in therapeutic settings, not to mention the increased child motivation and generalization that result from active participation in everyday routines with primary caregivers. Thus, the main purpose of this book is to provide a vehicle for empowering caregivers to implement ABA interventions within the context of their naturally occurring routines so that they can tap into the multitude of learning opportunities these contexts provide for all children. It is my hope that the procedures, tools, and strategies provided in this book will help practitioners bring intensive ABA interventions into the everyday experiences of children and families to optimize child development and increase home, school, and community inclusion.

Overview of Natural Environment Intervention

· ·

This chapter provides an overview of the use of natural environment intervention (NEI) for young children with disabilities. Coverage of the topic includes NEI's legal foundations and a review of literature on the principles of effective practice when implementing NEI. An overview of autism spectrum disorder (ASD) is offered, together with a discussion of research specifically related to NEI for young children with ASD.

NATURAL ENVIRONMENT INTERVENTION

NEI is a federally mandated early intervention approach for young children with disabilities that systematically maximizes teaching and learning opportunities throughout the day by embedding interventions within naturally occurring routines. Caregivers spend many hours with their child throughout the day, and this time can and should be used for interventions that will enhance the child's development. In using NEI, caregivers are not required to set aside extra time in their day to provide "therapy." Instead, they receive training and support from professionals to provide evidence-based interventions within the context of their daily routines. Thus, NEI doesn't require extra time, but it does require a more systematic use of time spent with the child to optimize learning opportunities throughout the day.

According to federal special education law (Part C of the Individuals with Disabilities Education Improvement Act [IDEA]), natural environments are defined as home and community settings in which children without disabilities participate

(IDEIA, 2004). The law requires that early intervention services for infants and toddlers with disabilities be implemented in natural environments to the maximum extent appropriate. This stipulation reflects research indicating that everyday family and community routines and activities provide young children with an optimal variety of learning opportunities (Dunst, Hamby, Trivette, Raab, & Bruder, 2000). Natural environments include a variety of home-, school-, and community-based routines. Examples of home-based routines may include dressing, bathing, eating, cleaning the house, playing outdoors or inside, and reading books. Community-based routines may include going to the grocery store, beach, library, and park. School-based routines may include circle time, lunch, centers, recess, library, small-group instruction, and whole-group instruction. These everyday home, school, and community routines provide young children with many different learning opportunities. When children are actively engaged in everyday routines, they have multiple opportunities to apply their existing skills and acquire new ones.

The National Association for the Education of Young Children (NAEYC), the world's largest organization working on behalf of young children, uses the developmentally appropriate practice (DAP) framework as the foundation of all its work. The core principles of DAP in early childhood education are that knowledge must inform decision making, goals must be challenging and achievable, and teaching must be intentional to be effective (NAEYC, 2012). These guiding principles also provide the framework for NEI through all phases of intervention, including assessment, goal setting, designing and implementing instruction, and evaluating the effects of instruction. When applying DAP to NEI for young children with disabilities, caregivers are heavily involved in the assessment process to identify the child's strengths, interests, everyday routines, and present abilities and needs so that early intervention teams are equipped with knowledge about the child and family. The team works collaboratively with caregivers to set goals based on what the child can currently do and what the child can be challenged to achieve next. Finally, with NEI, instruction is carefully designed using research-supported strategies to intentionally utilize everyday routines to maximize learning by embedding effective instruction within natural contexts. NEI and DAP differ in that NEI focuses on providing specific strategies and suggestions for how to intervene with young children during their everyday routines, whereas DAP provides more general guidelines for interacting with young children (Pretti-Frontczak & Bricker, 2004).

RESEARCH ON NATURAL ENVIRONMENT INTERVENTION

Professionals must think of NEI as involving not only *where* but *how* services are provided (Shelden & Rush, 2001). NEI is often misinterpreted as solely focusing on inclusion with typically developing peers rather than on the benefits of inclusive environments for interventions with young children with disabilities (Chai, Zhang, & Bisberg, 2006). Thus, it is essential for caregivers and early intervention providers to understand that NEI is not just about including young children with disabilities in naturally occurring everyday routines and activities but also about planning and implementing purposeful interventions within those contexts.

Researchers have conceptualized the delivery of NEI in a variety of ways to guide early intervention providers in their service delivery. Dunst and colleagues (2001) describe NEI as contextually based, child-initiated, and adult-directed learning opportunities provided by caregivers and mediated by professionals. In other words, professionals should recognize the natural learning opportunities that occur in a child's daily life and use those opportunities to implement interventions. NEI strongly emphasizes tapping into children's interests to increase their active participation in everyday activities (Dunst, Trivette, & Masiello, 2011).

Robin McWilliam (2010) uses an NEI model that revolves around the use of routines-based interviews (RBIs). RBIs are semistructured interviews that early intervention providers conduct with caregivers to determine the main concerns of the family, the family's everyday routines, the extent of the child's participation in everyday routines, the family's satisfaction during each of the routines, and the family's desired outcomes related to child-level needs, child-related family needs, and family-level needs. In a study comparing individualized family service plan (IFSP) outcomes using the RBI versus the business-as-usual IFSP development process, the outcomes written as a result of the RBI were more functional than outcomes written as a result of the standard process (McWilliam, Casey, & Sims, 2009).

Diane Bricker (2001) suggests that naturalistic teaching approaches, such as activity-based interventions (ABI), can be used across a range of settings to address a child's goals and objectives by implementing interventions during daily routines and activities. The ABI approach capitalizes on the child's motivation and the use of daily activities to embed multiple, varied, and authentic learning opportunities. ABI focuses on the attainment of functional skills that can be used across environments and situations (Pretti-Frontczak & Bricker, 2004).

While there are a variety of approaches to NEI, these approaches share several features. Using a family-centered approach that is individualized, strength based, capacity building, and reflective of the family's culture and values is the foundation of all NEI approaches (Atkins-Burnett & Allen-Meares, 2000; Woods, Wilcox, Friedman, & Murch, 2011). Providing ongoing coaching to caregivers to deliver the level of support they need to effectively implement interventions in the natural environment is an essential component of NEI, regardless of the approach used (Rush, Shelden, & Hanft, 2003). Using evidence-based methods and strategies to promote the child's development during naturally occurring family and community routines and activities is also a common emphasis of the NEI approaches.

NATURAL ENVIRONMENT INTERVENTION FOR YOUNG CHILDREN WITH ASD

Before discussing how to apply NEI for young children with ASD and related disorders, an overview of ASD will be provided for the benefit of readers who may not be familiar with ASD. It is crucial for early intervention providers to understand the characteristics of young children with ASD so they can address the children's core impairments within the context of NEI.

Overview of Autism Spectrum Disorders

The term ASD often is used quite loosely. You may hear some people say that a child doesn't have autism but is definitely on the spectrum. If a child has some characteristics associated with autism, it does not necessarily mean the child is on the spectrum. A child who is on the autism spectrum either has autism, Asperger syndrome, or pervasive developmental disorder-not otherwise specified (PDD-NOS). These three disorders are the only autism spectrum disorders. They belong to the larger category of pervasive developmental disorders (PDD), which also includes Rett syndrome and childhood disintegrative disorder (CDD), according to the *Diagnostic and Statistical Manual of Mental Disorders, Fourth Edition, Text Revision* (*DSM-IV-TR;* APA, 2000). For the purposes of this book, characteristics of children with ASD will be discussed without pinpointing the differences among these disorders.

Before discussing the impairments that children with ASD are likely to display, it is important to stress that children with ASD all possess unique strengths and talents. Because ASDs are neurological disorders, the brains of people with ASD are not necessarily "wired" the same way as in typically developing individuals. Thus, children with ASD may be able to do many things that most of their peers cannot do. Some children with ASD learn literacy skills such as letter and sound recognition and early sight word recognition well before their same-age typically developing peers. Some young children with ASD have extraordinary visual-spatial strengths that allow them to complete puzzles, use shape sorters, and engage in other constructive play activities that are designed for children who are much older. Children with ASD may also have special talents related to music and art. While not every young child with ASD will have a special talent, all children have strengths and interests that should be tapped into when planning interventions. Caregivers and early intervention providers should focus on and value these strengths rather than solely targeting children's impairments. With that said, the impairments of young children with ASD must be assessed and addressed to enable them to actively participate in home, school, and community routines and make developmental gains.

Impairments in Social Interaction   Children with ASD all have impairments in social interaction. However, not all children will have the same types of difficulties. Some children may have impairments in the use of nonverbal behaviors such as eye contact, facial expressions, body posture, and social gestures. Children with ASD may not spontaneously seek opportunities to interact with other people. This does not necessarily mean that these children "prefer to be alone," which is a descriptive characteristic that may be seen on a variety of informational materials related to ASD. When children with ASD receive the supports they need to learn how to respond to the initiations of others, to initiate interactions with others, and to maintain interactions with others, they may prefer social interactions to being alone. These skills related to interacting with others are referred to as joint attention and social reciprocity skills, which are core impairments in children with ASD (Jones & Carr, 2004; MacDonald et al., 2006; Mundy, 1995).

Joint attention entails two or more individuals sharing attention with one another related to a specific object, activity, or idea. Joint attention can consist of coordinating attention between people and objects, attending to a social partner, shifting gaze between people and objects, sharing emotional states with another person, and being able to draw another person's attention to objects or events for the purpose of sharing experiences (Baldwin, 1995; Mundy, Sigman, & Kasari, 1990). This type of interaction can be as simple as a child pointing to a bird in the tree with the caregiver responding, "Oh, wow! It's a blue jay!" Joint attention skills are also needed to engage in more complex social interactions. A basic way to understand joint attention is to think of it as the feeling that you are "in it together" that you might get when interacting with someone. Even when you try hard to interact and connect with a child on the autism spectrum, you may not feel the same sense of connectedness that you experience with typically developing children.

Once a child with ASD is connected with someone by establishing joint attention, the child then needs to use social reciprocity skills to engage in "the dance of human interaction," which involves long chains of back-and-forth interactions related to the object, activity, or idea in which they are sharing attention. Social reciprocity entails being aware of the emotional and interpersonal cues of others, appropriately interpreting those cues, responding appropriately to what is interpreted, and being motivated to engage in social interactions with others (Constantino et al., 2003). Below is an example of social reciprocity being shared between a mother and her 2-year-old daughter, Rebecca.

Mother: It's time for breakfast, Rebecca.

(Rebecca walks over to the kitchen table and stands by her booster seat.)

Mother: Do you want to get in your chair?

Rebecca: Help me up.

(Mother picks up Rebecca and puts her in her chair.)

Rebecca: I want pancakes.

Mother: Okay. Do you want bananas with your pancakes?

Rebecca: Yes.

(Mother gives Rebecca pancakes and bananas.)

In this example Rebecca and her mother shared many back-and-forth exchanges. Notice that some exchanges were not verbal but were actions conducted in response to the initiation or response of the other person. That is still a reciprocal exchange. Exchanges can be verbal or can entail the use of facial expressions, gestures, or actions. Also, social reciprocity entails making initiations and responding to the initiations of others. In the example provided, Rebecca was able to respond to her mother's initiations (i.e., "It's time for breakfast"), and she also initiated an interaction ("I want pancakes"). Although social reciprocity skills develop naturally in typically developing children, children with ASD often require intensive interventions to learn how to engage in reciprocal social interactions.

Impairments in Communication   Children with ASD may have difficulty sending information and receiving information when interacting with communication partners. To engage in reciprocal social interactions, individuals need to use nonverbal and verbal receptive and expressive communication skills. Nonverbal communication can entail the use of eye contact, facial expressions, body posture, social gestures, actions, and the ability to interpret nonverbal behaviors displayed by others. Verbal communication skills can entail responding to or initiating interactions with others through the use of verbal responses, sign language, picture exchange, or augmentative communication devices. Expressive language skills consist of the use of language to share knowledge, thoughts, and ideas with others. When children have impairments in expressive communication, they may have difficulty expressing their wants and needs, commenting, answering and asking questions, and engaging in conversations. When children with ASD do use expressive language, their words may be difficult to understand due to poor articulation. They may have trouble using appropriate volume, or they may display irregular prosody that may result in sounding nasal or robotic. Receptive language skills consist of demonstrating understanding of language. When children have impairments in receptive communication, they may have difficulty responding to directions that require comprehension of language that is beyond their level of understanding.

Typically developing children supplement verbal communication with nonverbal communication by using gestures, eye contact, facial expressions, and body posture to send messages to others. Many children with disabilities who lack verbal communication skills often use even more of these nonverbal communication skills to compensate for their lack of verbal skills, but children with ASD often do not do this. In fact, many times their lack of nonverbal communication skills sends the wrong message to their communication partners. For example, many children with ASD do not use appropriate eye contact when speaking with others. That may send the message that they are not talking to someone in particular when in fact they are. Also, if they do not use facial expressions to communicate their thoughts and feelings, they may be misinterpreted as being disengaged or uninterested when that is not the case. When children engage with their peers, many times it is nonverbal communication such as eye contact, gestures, and facial expressions that help them connect with one another. Thus, children with ASD often miss out on opportunities to establish connections with peers due to their limited nonverbal communication skills.

Some children with ASD may display stereotyped and repetitive use of language, which encompasses a variety of idiosyncratic uses of language. This can include echolalia, or repeating what was heard previously in exactly the same way at a later time. Echolalia is often considered a nonfunctional use of language; however, a child with ASD may use echolalia as a means of communication. For example, a 3-year-old girl with autism engaged in echolalia at dismissal from preschool by repeatedly saying,

"Dirty. Take a bath." The teacher and the parents were eager to get her to stop this "nonfunctional" use of language. However, the early interventionist hypothesized that the little girl was saying that phrase repeatedly because she always wore pretty dresses and didn't want to sit on the sidewalk during dismissal time because it would mean getting her dress dirty. The early interventionist suggested that instead of asking the child to sit on the sidewalk with the other students, the teacher might provide a chair for her to sit in while she waited to be picked up. When this change was made, the child stopped saying, "Dirty. Take a bath." This shows that her echolalia was actually serving a communicative function. She didn't have the expressive language skills to say, "I don't want to sit on the sidewalk because I don't want my dress to get dirty," so she used a phrase she often heard her mother say at home when she was dirty. Some children may use echolalia because they want to interact with others but do not have the social communication skills needed to initiate an interaction. Thus, they use echolalia to attempt to initiate interactions with others. Other children with ASD may have verbal self-stimulatory behaviors, or stims, in which they verbalize certain sounds, words, phrases, or sentences in a nonfunctional manner. Often children who use verbal stims do so when they are not engaged in a meaningful interaction or activity. Therefore, it is important to get children actively engaged when they do begin to use verbal stims as opposed to simply trying to stop the behavior from occurring.

Restricted Interests and Repetitive Behaviors   According to the _DSM-IV-TR_ (APA, 2000), an individual with ASD has at least one of the following characteristics:

- Restricted range of interests; intense fascination with a particular interest

- Need for sameness; repetitive routines

- Self-stimulatory motor movements

- Strong interest in objects or parts of objects

The first indicator refers to children with ASD who have a special interest in something that limits the individual's capacity for a variety of interests. For example, a child may have a passion for trains and only want to play with trains and talk about trains. Some individuals with ASD will have a need for sameness in which they have a strong urge for certain things to be done a certain way each time. For example, a child may have a strong desire to follow a specific routine before bedtime by reading a specific book followed by singing a specific song, and even the slightest change in that routine may cause the child to engage in challenging behaviors. It is best to teach children who have these needs for sameness how to handle small changes as opposed to "walking on eggshells" to keep them from getting upset.

Stereotyped and repetitive movements can include behaviors such as rocking, hand flapping, spinning objects, lining things up, or any other movement that the child displays often without a functional purpose. Some children with ASD are interested in parts of objects such as wheels on a toy car. Thus, when they pick up a toy car they do not necessarily play with it as other children might play, but instead they focus on spinning and examining the wheels and exploring how they work. These types of stereotyped behaviors usually occur when the child is disengaged from meaningful activities, as was discussed with verbal self-stimulatory behaviors. Thus, it is crucial to positively redirect children to engaging activities when these behaviors arise as opposed to simply trying to get children to stop doing them.

Other Characteristics of Young Children with ASD   In addition to impairments in social interaction, impairments in communication, and the presence of stereotypic behaviors and/or restricted interests, some children with ASD may have a variety of other challenges. Some additional challenges that children with ASD and their families may face include extreme anxiety and fear, sensory sensitivities, food allergies, sleep disorders, gastrointestinal issues, attention difficulties, feeding disorders, severe challenging behaviors, seizures, cognitive impairments, fine motor difficulties, and gross motor difficulties. Because caregivers of young children with ASD may be dealing with a wide range of challenges, it is essential for early intervention providers to assess what challenges exist and develop interventions that caregivers can implement to address specific challenges.

Autism Variability

It is important for readers to understand that even though children with ASD share common characteristics, there is great variability in the profiles of these children. A profile is a pattern of characteristics along several dimensions that distinguishes one child with autism from another in important ways (Thompson, 2011). Travis Thompson (2011) discussed autism variability in great detail in his book *Individualized Autism Intervention for Young Children: Blending Discrete Trial and Naturalistic Strategies.* It is well documented that children with ASD have impairments in social interaction and communication skills and that they are likely to engage in nonfunctional repetitive behaviors or have a restricted range of interests. Thompson discussed factors that moderate or intensify the expression of these autism symptoms including the child's intellectual ability, language skills, attention deficit and hyperactivity symptoms, and anxiety challenges. Each child's profile should be thoroughly examined when planning early intervention services and supports to ensure appropriate individualization to address the unique needs of each child.

Rationale for Using Natural Environment Interaction with Young Children with ASD

Although young children with ASD and their families face many challenges, there is mounting evidence demonstrating the effectiveness of intensive early intervention for a substantial proportion of these children (National Research Council, 2001; Woods & Wetherby, 2003). In 2001, the National Research Council (NRC) conducted a review of research on educational interventions for children with ASD from birth through age 8. Following a thorough literature review, the council identified the essential active ingredients of effective interventions for children with ASD. According to Wetherby and Woods (2006), the essential active ingredients suggested by the NRC (2001) that specifically support the effectiveness of NEI include the following:

1. Children must learn functional and meaningful skills.

2. Learning should occur within daily caregiving, play, and social interactions with caregivers that are repeated throughout the day.

3. Caregivers should mediate the teaching and learning process for the child as it occurs.

In the years following the NRC recommendations, researchers implemented studies examining the effects of NEI on young children with ASD. Today there is a growing body of evidence supporting caregiver-implemented interventions in the natural environment for young children with ASD. A study of five preschool children with autism showed that parents were able to demonstrate proficient use of evidence-based teaching strategies during their everyday routines (Kashinath, Woods, & Goldstein, 2006). A study of 17 children with ASD using a parent-implemented intervention that trained parents to embed naturalistic teaching strategies in their everyday routines showed that the children made significant gains in social communication skills as a result of the interventions (Wetherby & Woods, 2006). A study of preschoolers with autism showed that when children were engaged in interest-based activities during everyday family and community activities they made more progress in language, social, and motor development than children with autism who did not engage in interest-based activities (Dunst, Trivette, & Masiello, 2011). Project DATA (Developmentally Appropriate Treatment for Autism), an inclusive preschool program for children with ASD between 1 year and 3 years old, shows positive outcome data of teachers using evidence-based instructional strategies to embed instruction into the ongoing classroom routines and activities to improve social communication skills, cognitive development, and self-regulation skills (Boulware, Schwartz, Sandall, & McBride, 2006).

What Is Unique about Natural Environment Interaction for Young Children with ASD?

The use of NEI for young children with ASD is somewhat controversial because of the documented need for intensive interventions among this population of children. Since 1987, with Lovaas' landmark study of discrete trial training (DTT; see Chapter 2), there has been a push toward providing 40 hours per week of one-to-one DTT professionally driven therapy for children with ASD. There is a general belief among some caregivers and professionals that children with ASD cannot learn during naturally occurring home and community routines in the way typically developing children do. While it is true that children with ASD often do not learn in the same way that typically developing children do and require alternative instructional strategies, it does not mean that children with ASD cannot learn during everyday routines. What it does mean is that children with ASD require specialized interventions to be implemented during their everyday routines to enable them to learn from those natural experiences.

In contrast with the 40-hours-of-DTT-per-week formula, the NRC (2001) recommended that children with ASD receive at least 25 hours each week of active engagement in intensive instructional programming. Many caregivers and professionals mistakenly interpret that recommendation to mean that the child should receive at least 25 hours of one-to-one instruction in therapeutic or clinical settings each week. To the contrary, with carefully designed NEI, young children can receive the intensity of interventions they need within their ongoing routines across home, school, and community settings. Of course, some children may require one-to-one ABA interventions in addition to NEI, depending on the profiles of the children. For example, if a child has moderate to severe cognitive impairments, severe language impairments, severe social impairments, severe attention-related difficulties, and/or severe anxiety issues, the child may need some therapeutic ABA interventions to address these difficulties and to enable the child to fully benefit from NEI.

So, what is unique about the way NEI must be designed for young children with ASD? First, using an interest-based approach to increasing the child's active participation in everyday routines is essential. At the same time, the skills that are targeted for intervention during those routines must address the child's core impairments. Specifically, joint attention, social reciprocity, and communication skills must continually be targeted during NEI for young children with ASD.

Second, the instructional strategies selected for use within everyday routines must have an evidence base specifically for children with ASD. Intervention approaches that utilize principles of applied behavior analysis (ABA) have a strong research base for their effectiveness with young children with ASD (Koegel, Koegel, Harrower, & Carter, 1999; Lovaas, 1987; McGee, Morrier, & Daly, 1999; Pierce & Schreibman, 1997). Contrary to some misconceptions of caregivers and professionals, ABA teaching strategies can and should be implemented within naturally occurring everyday routines as opposed to one-to-one settings that remove the child from the natural environment. Some of the drawbacks of one-to-one ABA therapy include difficulties with child motivation and with generalization of learned skills. In contrast, when young children are actively engaged in NEI, they have increased motivation due to the emphasis on the children's interests and participation in familiar and preferred routines; and generalization is less of a difficulty due to the fact that children are learning functional and meaningful skills in the very contexts where they are expected to use them.

Finally, planning for at least 25 hours each week of NEI is essential for young children with ASD. Children with mild developmental delays may not necessarily need the intensity of at least 25 hours of intervention each week. Because children with ASD need this intensity, however, early intervention teams must consider this requirement when conducting assessments and planning interventions.

CHAPTER SUMMARY

This chapter has provided an overview of NEI and described how it can be applied to young children with ASD. It is not just suggested that early intervention providers use NEI; it is federally mandated. Early intervention providers can guide their NEI practices by familiarizing themselves with a wealth of literature that encourages family-centered practices and provides guidelines for coaching caregivers as they learn to implement interventions during their everyday home and community routines using evidence-based practices. The use of NEI for young children with ASD must meaningfully address their core impairments in social interaction and communication, utilize ABA teaching principles, and provide at least 25 hours each week of active engagement in intensive instructional programming.

2

Understanding Applied
Behavior Analysis

· ·

This chapter introduces the field of applied behavior analysis (ABA), providing a brief overview of behaviorism and discussing how it paved the way for ABA. Coverage includes the seven dimensions of ABA and ways to meet these dimensions in the natural environment. Specific applications of ABA in working with young children with ASD are briefly discussed, including discrete trial training, pivotal response treatment, incidental teaching, and applied verbal behavior. The chapter concludes with a discussion of how ABA can be implemented in the natural environment to meet the needs of children with ASD.

BRIEF OVERVIEW OF BEHAVIORISM

Applied behavior analysis (ABA) is based on principles of behaviorism, a theory of learning based on the idea that all behaviors are learned through conditioning. Behaviorism identifies two forms of conditioning: classical conditioning and operant conditioning. Classical conditioning entails pairing a neutral stimulus with a naturally occurring stimulus to get the same response for the neutral stimulus that is evoked from the natural stimulus. In the early 1900s, Ivan Pavlov experimented with classical conditioning in his studies with dogs. The natural stimulus was food and the response was salivation: The dogs would salivate when presented with food. Pavlov was able to show how to achieve the same response with a different stimulus by pairing. Each time the dogs were presented with food, a bell would ring and the dogs would salivate. Eventually, when the bell rang even without the presence of food, the dogs still salivated. Thus, the dogs were conditioned to salivate whenever they heard a bell ring.

Operant conditioning, based on the work of B.F. Skinner, is a method of learning through rewards and punishment. From the 1930s to the 1950s, Skinner conducted many studies to show the effects of environmental consequences on behaviors. One of his most famous studies entailed using positive reinforcement to teach pigeons to peck on a lever. Each time the pigeons pecked on the lever, a pellet of food was dispensed. Thus, the pigeons learned to increase their behavior of pecking on the lever to get food.

ABA expands the use of experimental behavioral conditioning beyond laboratories and animals to encompass natural environments and people. Thus, ABA is the science of applying principles of behaviorism to make meaningful changes in the lives of individuals. The science of ABA provides a proactive approach for teaching new skills and addressing problem behaviors. This entails setting specific, observable, measurable goals that are meaningful across contexts, designing explicitly detailed behavioral interventions to teach the skills required to achieve the goals, and monitoring progress through ongoing data collection and analysis.

HISTORY OF APPLIED BEHAVIOR ANALYSIS

The field of ABA was "born" in 1968 when Baer, Wolf, and Risley published their landmark paper, "Some Current Dimensions of Applied Behavior Analysis," in the first volume of the *Journal of Applied Behavior Analysis*. In this paper, they presented a framework for conducting applied behavior analytic research. Their framework consisted of seven dimensions that had to be present for single-subject research to be considered ABA. Today, this framework is also used for implementing ABA intervention programs that are not designed for research purposes. Whether ABA is used for research or daily intervention programs, it continues to be defined by these seven dimensions:

1. Applied

2. Behavioral

3. Analytic

4. Conceptual

5. Technological

6. Effective

7. Generality

Each dimension is discussed in detail and also summarized in Table 2.1.

Applied

An intervention is *applied* if it has immediate face validity—that is, if it solves an important problem (Baer, Wolf, & Risley, 1968; Baer, Wolf, & Risley, 1987; Bailey &

Burch, 2002). In other words, *applied* means that the intervention is implemented to make meaningful changes in the life of an individual. This expectation is met by setting appropriate goals for the ABA interventions (see Chapter 4). Goals that are set for young children with ASD sometimes are not meaningful for the child. For example, one-on-one ABA programs may include goals such as imitating block designs, matching two-dimensional objects to three-dimensional objects, or matching an object to the appropriate category. These types of goals may not necessarily have meaning to the child across a variety of natural contexts or enhance the quality of life for the child and the family. Instead, goals can be designed that will address the communication and social interaction impairments of children with ASD, such as imitating peers in play, pointing to pictures of desired items to make requests, or describing an experience using a complete sentence. When goals such as these are mastered, they are useful across a variety of settings and enhance the child's ability to engage with others.

Behavioral

Behavioral means that the goal set for the ABA intervention must be observable and measurable. If the goal is observable, it focuses on what the child actually does, as observed and recorded by another person (Baer, Wolf, & Risley, 1968; Baer, Wolf, & Risley, 1987; Bailey & Burch, 2002). A nonexample of an observable goal would be one stating that the child will be happy. Happiness is not necessarily something that can be seen. While some people may clearly show happiness by smiling or laughing, the happiness of others may not be as obvious. Instead, an observable goal could be defined by stating that the child will make eye contact with a peer when the peer joins the child in play.

If the goal is measurable, that means different people can collect data on child performance in the same way. This is achieved by clearly defining the behavioral expectation. A goal stating that the child will participate on the playground is insufficiently defined because different adults are likely to measure participation in different ways. Participation may mean joining another child in a play area, asking another child to play, engaging in reciprocal interactions with another child during a play activity, independently using the playground equipment, or displaying other behaviors. Thus, when writing a goal, it is important to clearly define the behaviors that will be required to fulfill the expectation.

Analytic

Analytic means that there is a functional relationship between the procedures implemented and the actual behavioral change (Baer, Wolf, & Risley, 1968; Baer, Wolf, & Risley, 1987; Bailey & Burch, 2002). In other words, the interventions being implemented with the child are responsible for the changes in behavior. In a research design, this can be shown in a variety of ways, such as through multiple-baseline designs, reversal designs, and repeated measures. These research methods involve systematically collecting data to demonstrate that the intervention is responsible for the changes in behavior. However, when implementing ABA in the natural environment for intervention purposes as opposed to research purposes, it is somewhat difficult to fulfill this dimension of ABA. Typically, teaching designs are used when implementing daily behavioral interventions. Teaching designs consist of taking baseline data and intervention data only. Realistically this is as far as interventionists are usually able to go to document that the intervention is responsible for the change in behavior.

So, to meet the *analytic* dimension of ABA, it is important for interventionists to at least collect baseline data before beginning any ABA intervention. If baseline data are not collected, it is difficult to know whether the intervention is responsible for the change in behavior. Also, taking baseline data allows interventionists to determine whether the intervention is having a positive effect. For example, if a child is displaying tantrum behaviors when making the transition from playing outside to going inside for dinner, parents and interventionists may try a specific strategy to reduce the tantrums and increase the child's ability to transition appropriately. If baseline data are collected, the team can compare intervention data with the baseline data to determine whether the intervention is working. Without this comparison, parents may stop implementing an intervention because they believe it is not working. Even if the tantrums are still occurring, if they are occurring less frequently or with less intensity than during baseline, the intervention should continue until the desirable outcome is reached.

Conceptual

Conceptual means that the teaching procedures being used as part of an intervention are based on principles of behaviorism (Baer, Wolf, & Risley, 1968; Baer, Wolf, & Risley, 1987; Bailey & Burch, 2002). This may entail the use of positive reinforcement procedures, prompting/fading procedures, shaping, time-delay, behavioral momentum, task analysis, or extinction, to name a few techniques. Chapter 5 provides detailed descriptions of these strategies and others, including definitions and examples.

To meet the *conceptual* dimension of ABA, the teaching procedures must utilize strategies that have been shown effective through behavioral research. A teaching procedure may be quite effective, but if it does not include the use of behavioral teaching strategies, it is not an ABA intervention. For example, a child might learn to say, "All done!" when she has finished eating by hearing her sister say the same thing. In such a case the peer modeling is an effective teaching procedure but it is not an ABA intervention because no specific behavioral strategies were used. However, if the modeling of her sister is not enough for the child to learn to say "All done!" and the parent must use prompting/fading procedures to teach the child to do so, then the intervention is *conceptual* since it entails the use of at least one behavioral strategy.

Technological

The *technological* dimension of ABA has nothing to do with what most people think of when they hear the word "technology." Instead, it means that the teaching procedures are written in such a clear, explicit manner that any person implementing the procedures would use exactly the same methods (Baer, Wolf, & Risley, 1968; Baer, Wolf, & Risley, 1987; Bailey & Burch, 2002). The key word here is "written." It is very difficult to meet the technological requirement without writing the teaching procedures down. Although a group of individuals implementing an ABA intervention can meet to discuss how the teaching will be conducted, it is unlikely that these discussions alone will result in each person implementing the intervention in exactly the same way. Thus, it is best to put the procedures in writing so that everyone can refer to them. Chapter 5 provides examples of ABA intervention plans that are written to meet the technological dimension, and Appendixes A through F provide additional sample intervention plans. It can be time-consuming to write teaching procedures when you begin implementing ABA interventions. Therefore, these samples provide a bank of teaching procedures you can use with children to reduce the time spent on developing teaching procedures. Of course, you will have to modify the teaching procedures to meet the individual needs of each child, and there will be goals you want to address that are not included in the samples. However, you will find that once you gain experience writing the procedures, it becomes easier and easier to develop *technological* teaching procedures.

Effective

Effective means that the intervention being used is making meaningful and significant changes for the child (Baer, Wolf, & Risley, 1968; Baer, Wolf, & Risley, 1987; Bailey & Burch, 2002). How do we determine what is considered significant change? Baer, Wolf, and Risley (1968) suggested asking yourself the following question: How much did the specific behavior need to be changed? For example, if you were implementing an intervention to improve positive social interactions with peers and reduce aggressive behaviors toward peers, the aggression would need to diminish greatly for the intervention to be considered effective. If a child hits other children 20 times per week during baseline and only reduces the hitting to 15 times per week after the intervention is implemented, that is not enough behavior change for the intervention to be considered effective. The child would need to drastically reduce aggression toward peers for the intervention to be considered effective. If the child reduces the number of aggressive acts toward peers each week from 20 to 5, it is probably safe to say that the intervention is effective. Of course, the intervention would continue until the aggressive acts are diminished completely.

The *effective* dimension is where the data analysis comes into play. Many times interventionists collect data when implementing ABA interventions. However, just collecting data is not enough. Interventionists must analyze the data to make instructional decisions. The best way to do this is to create a graphical display of the data you are collecting. You cannot analyze your data by leafing through pages and pages of data sheets collected in a binder of some sort. For each goal, you should create a graphical display of the child's progress. Then you must examine the data to determine whether the child is making adequate progress. Chapter 6 describes a variety of ways to collect and graph data and outlines procedures for interpreting data in order to make instructional decisions.

In research designs, *effective* also pertains to reliability. This means that the intervention being used has been shown to have positive effects with a variety of individuals across a variety of different contexts and situations. Simply put, an intervention is reliable when it is implemented repeatedly with different individuals and the results are positive for all or most of the individuals receiving the intervention. This goes hand-in-hand with the *conceptual* dimension. Research has shown the reliability of interventions designed for children with ASD that utilize principles of behaviorism such as positive reinforcement, shaping, prompting/fading procedures, behavioral momentum, and time-delay (Davis, Brady, Hamilton, McEvoy, & Williams, 1994; Lovaas, 1987; McGee, Almeida, Sulzer-Azaroff, & Feldman, 1992; Pierce & Schreibman, 1995). Thus, ABA interventions utilize these strategies because of their consistent reliability, and that is why they are part of the *conceptual* framework of ABA teaching procedures.

Generality

Generality means that the skills the child learns are used across a variety of contexts and situations. The ability of children with ASD to generalize what they learn is often documented as inadequate (Gresham & MacMillan, 1998). Therefore, educators must carefully plan to teach children how to generalize the skills they are learning as opposed to just hoping they will do so. If ABA intervention programs meet the *applied* dimension and develop goals that are meaningful for the child across a variety of contexts, it is much easier to plan for generalization. For example, if the goal consists of teaching a child to greet others, the teaching procedures can be implemented in the home, in the grocery store, at the park, and at the preschool. Another way to plan for generalization is to do what Stokes and Baer (1977) called "train loosely". This means varying the ways that you present requests to children so they learn how to respond no matter how a request is made. This also means accepting a variety of appropriate responses from the child instead of teaching only one specific response. Below is a scenario that clearly illustrates the importance of training loosely when working with children with ASD:

> Brian, a 5-year-old boy with autism, was learning how to respond to greetings. The intervention being used was very specific. The adult would say, "Hi, Brian!" and Brian would then have to say, "Hi," followed by the adult's name. Well, one day Brian was at the community park with his mother. A stranger wearing a yellow shirt said, "Hello!" to Brian. While it was great that Brian knew to respond even though the woman said "hello" and not "hi," it wasn't so great that he said, "Hi . . . yellow" because he didn't know the woman's name. He knew the right response was to say "hi" and then the name, so he came up with the closest thing he could think of. The resulting greeting was quite humorous and also a perfect example of why there shouldn't be highly specific expectations for responses. Instead, Brian should have learned that he could say "hi" and the person's name or just "hi" or "hello" or "hey" or any other appropriate greeting.

Table 2.1 summarizes the seven dimensions of ABA interventions.

Table 2.1. Dimensions of applied behavior analysis

Dimension	Explanation
Applied	The intervention is designed to have a meaningful, positive impact on the life of the child.
Behavioral	The goal can be directly observed and measured. The objective is defined so clearly that different people can measure the behavior in the same way.
Analytical	Data show that the intervention is responsible for the change in behavior.
Conceptual	Interventions utilize research-based behavioral teaching strategies.
Technological	The teaching procedures are written so explicitly that different individuals can implement them in the same manner.
Effective	The intervention results in significant positive changes in behavior.
Generality	The skills learned can be maintained over time and utilized across different settings and contexts.

APPLICATIONS OF ABA FOR CHILDREN WITH ASD

During the late 1970s, researchers began applying ABA to children with ASD. A variety of specific applications of ABA have been developed since then to help children with ASD learn. The following section provides an overview of a few of these applications of ABA for children with ASD, including discrete trial training, pivotal response treatment, incidental teaching, and applied verbal behavior. These are the most common ABA approaches used in working with children who have ASD, and it is important for interventionists to understand these valuable teaching methods in order to learn how to utilize them in appropriate ways in the natural environment.

Discrete Trial Training

Discrete trial training (DTT) is an ABA approach that entails breaking down skills into discrete tasks and using structured behavioral teaching to ensure mastery of each task (Lovaas, 1987). DTT uses an A-B-C teaching format. The A, or antecedent, represents an opportunity for the child to respond to a specific stimulus. The antecedent may be a question, a direction, a comment, a gesture, or any other stimulus that would require a response. The B, or behavior, is an appropriate response to the antecedent that the child displays. The C, or consequence, is positive reinforcement that is delivered following the appropriate behavior. Of course, if the child doesn't have the skill that is being taught, it is not likely that the child will be able to respond to the antecedent without some assistance. This assistance would be provided in the form of a prompt. A prompt is a cue that can be verbal, gestural, or physical. It is given following the antecedent to enable the child to successfully display the desired behavior. Then positive reinforcement is provided. Eventually the prompts are faded out until the child can respond without any prompts at all. With DTT, multiple learning opportunities, or trials, are presented to the child to promote learning mastery. These trials may be presented multiple times in a row. This is called mass trialing. However, multiple trials can be implemented throughout the child's day as well. The most important aspect of DTT is that it prevents empty requests from being made to children with ASD. Often interventionists will present an antecedent (question, comment, direction), but the child will not respond. This is an empty request unless the interventionist follows through to ensure a successful response. With DTT, by contrast, the interventionist delivers a prompt to enable the child to respond successfully and then provides positive reinforcement following the response. Embedded discrete trials is a strategy that will be discussed in Chapter 5. This strategy uses the A-B-C teaching sequence embedded within naturally occurring routines and activities. Other behavioral strategies used when implementing DTT, such as positive reinforcement, prompting/fading procedures, and shaping, will also be discussed in Chapter 5. In the following example, a mother is using DTT to teach her daughter, Allison, to turn the page of the book during a shared book reading activity:

(Mother reads a page of the book to Allison.)

Mother: Turn the page, Allison. (antecedent)

(Allison does not respond.)

Mother: Turn the page, Allison.

(Mother points to the page and pushes the book closer to Allison.)

(antecedent with a prompt)

(Allison turns the page.)

(Mother smiles and makes eye contact with Allison.)

Mother: Great job! Let's see what happens next!

(consequence-positive reinforcement)

Pivotal Response Treatment

Pivotal Response Treatment (PRT) is another ABA approach that provides structured teaching within the child's natural environment (Koegel, Koegel, Harrower, & Carter, 1999). Unlike DTT, PRT focuses on addressing five pivotal areas rather than breaking skills down into discrete tasks. This approach is based on the premise that when these five pivotal areas are targeted, changes occur in other untargeted areas (Koegel & Koegel, 1995). The five pivotal areas include motivation, responsivity to multiple cues, self-management, self-initiations, and empathy (Koegel et al., 1999). Family involvement is a critical component of PRT because interventions are implemented across the child's day in natural contexts in the home and community. Strategies that are used when implementing PRT include making environmental arrangements in natural contexts to create opportunities for social interaction and communication, following the child's lead to increase motivation, shaping by accepting all attempts and gradually improving the quality of responses, and providing natural reinforcement for attempts made by the child (Koegel & Koegel, 2006). These strategies are discussed in detail in Chapter 5. Utilizing these strategies and implementing intervention in the natural environment helps to ensure that the skills being learned are generalized across a variety of contexts. Here is an example of a father using PRT to teach his son, Alex, how to point to a desired item:

(Alex stands next to the kitchen counter and whines.)

(Father kneels down to get face-to-face with Alex, following the child's lead.)

Father: You must want something, Alex.

(Alex continues to whine.)

Father: Do you want your juice?

(Father models how to point to the juice cup.)

(Alex reaches for the juice cup, but does not point.)

Father: Here you go, Alex.

(Father gives Alex the juice cup as natural reinforcement and will work on teaching Alex to point instead of reach next time.)

Incidental Teaching

Incidental teaching (IT) is another ABA approach that uses natural contexts to promote the use of communication and social interaction (Hart & Risley, 1975). With IT, caregivers and interventionists follow the child's lead to create opportunities for the child to communicate in order to get wants and needs met. As is true with PRT, IT focuses on increasing initiations, enhancing motivation, and promoting generalization. Natural reinforcement, environmental arrangements, time-delay, prompting/fading procedures, and modeling/request imitation are strategies used when implementing IT (see Chapter 5 for descriptions of these strategies). Typically developing peers can be taught how to use IT and PRT to promote communication and social interaction with children with ASD (McGee, Almeida, Sulzer-Azaroff, & Feldman, 1992; Pierce & Schreibman, 1995; Pierce & Schreibman, 1997). The use of peer-mediated interventions such as these will be discussed in Chapter 5.

Applied Verbal Behavior

Applied verbal behavior (AVB) is an ABA approach that incorporates DTT but also relies on B.F. Skinner's classification of language (Skinner, 1957) to teach language acquisition. This entails first teaching children with ASD to request, label, imitate, and then engage in conversations. Based on Skinner's work, the terms used for these skills in AVB are mand, tact, echoic, intraverbal, textual, and transcriptive (Sundberg & Michael, 2001). There are some additional differences between DTT and AVB that have been clearly explained in an article in *The Behavior Analyst Today* (Kates-McElrath & Axelrod, 2006). In DTT, children often engage in escape-motivated behavior. In other words, they complete a task to get a break from the task. With AVB, the interventionist serves as a conditioned social reinforcer. This means that children are taught to enjoy the interactions they are having with the individual with whom they are working, as opposed to trying to get away from the interaction. Another difference between DTT and AVB is that while DTT is typically implemented in a one-to-one, distraction-free environment, AVB includes intervention in the natural environment or uses natural environment training (NET) in addition to intervention in a distraction-free environment to enhance motivation. DTT and AVB use different curriculum guides for goal selection. DTT uses curriculum developed by Lovaas and others as a scope and sequence (Lovaas, 2003; Lovaas et al., 1981; Maurice, Green, & Luce, 1996). AVB uses the *Assessment of Basic Language and Learning Skills-Revised* (ABLLS-R) assessment program developed by Partington (2007) as well as the *Verbal Behavior Milestones Assessment and Placement Program* (VB-MAPP) developed by Sundberg (2008).

Using ABA in the Natural Environment

A growing body of evidence supports the positive effects of caregivers implementing ABA in the natural environment during everyday routines with young children with ASD (Boulware, Schwartz, Sandall, & McBride, 2006; Kashinath, Woods, & Goldstein, 2006; Wetherby & Woods, 2006). The advantages of applying ABA interventions in natural contexts rather than therapeutic settings are many, including increased child motivation, increased generalization of learned skills, and increased competence and confidence of caregivers. When implementing ABA interventions in the natural environment, strategies from all of the different ABA approaches can be used in some way. However, this book does not encourage interventionists to select one specific ABA approach when planning a comprehensive ABA intervention program that will be implemented within naturally occurring routines and activities across home, school, and community settings. Goals must be individualized, developmentally appropriate, and meaningful for the child while addressing parental priorities. Therefore, using a prepackaged assessment and curriculum guide as the sole tool for designing ABA interventions may be limiting and may not fully address the needs of the child and family. Instead, interventionists can apply the seven dimensions of ABA to assess, set goals, design interventions, and monitor progress to meet the unique and diverse needs of the children and families they serve.

CHAPTER SUMMARY

This chapter has provided an overview of ABA, discussed several common ABA applications designed specifically for children with ASD, and concluded with a discussion of how ABA can be used in the natural environment to address the unique needs of young children with ASD and other disabilities. This book provides interventionists with a method of implementing ABA in the natural environment by discussing ways to select goals (*applied*), write objectives (*behavioral*), collect baseline and intervention data (*analytical*), develop clear, explicit teaching procedures that use research-based behavioral strategies (*conceptual* and *technological*), analyze the data to make instructional decisions (*effective*), and ensure that children learn how to apply skills across a variety of situations and contexts (*generality*). The chapters that follow will guide you through the assessment, goal setting, and intervention phases of planning and implementing ABA interventions within the natural environment in collaboration with caregivers and other professionals.

Assessment for Planning ABA Interventions in the Natural Environment

. . . .

This chapter provides step-by-step procedures for conducting assessments that lead to meaningful goal selection for ABA interventions implemented in the natural environment. A variety of assessment tools are provided for you to reproduce and use. The chapter begins by introducing a young boy named Andrew and his family. This child and his family are featured throughout the book to show sample assessments, goals, interventions, data sheets, and collaboration activities.

Meet Andrew

Andrew is a 2½-year-old boy who lives with his mom, dad, and his 4-year-old sister. He is interested in letters and words, enjoys playing with electronics such as iPods and iPads, and he loves his family a great deal. He actively participates in physical activities such as gym class, outdoor play, Hide and Seek, and jumping on a trampoline. Andrew was diagnosed with autism when he was 23 months old and began receiving ABA interventions at that time. At the onset of the interventions, Andrew was nonverbal, displayed limited joint attention, was unable to feed himself, rarely played appropriately with toys, and seemed to prefer to be alone. His mom, Jennifer, serves as the primary interventionist working with a behavior analyst to learn how to implement ABA interventions within the family's everyday routines. After 7 months of interventions, Andrew has begun speaking, plays with a variety of age-appropriate toys, is able to initiate joint attention, respond to initiations from others, maintain joint attention, demonstrate an expansive receptive vocabulary, imitate adults and peers, and feed himself independently. Recently he started attending a community preschool to gain more socialization experiences.

OVERVIEW OF ASSESSMENT FOR PLANNING ABA INTERVENTIONS IN THE NATURAL ENVIRONMENT

When you hear the word *assessment*, you may think of standardized tests, screening instruments, developmental scope and sequence checklists, and other formal evaluation tools. Early intervention teams may choose a variety of these formal assessment tools for young children with ASD to determine eligibility for services and to obtain information about the child's general performance levels to assist in goal setting. They may use norm-referenced assessments such as the Wechsler Preschool and Primary Scale of Intelligence (WPSSI; Wechsler, 2002), the Bayley Scales of Infant and Toddler Development, Third Edition (Bayley-III; Bayley, 2005), the Vineland Adaptive Behavior Scales-II (VABS-II; Sparrow, Cicchetti, & Balla, 2005), the Young Children's Achievement Test (YCAT; Hresko, Peak, Herron, & Bridges, 2000), the Social Communication Questionnaire (SCQ; Rutter, Bailey, & Lord, 2003), and the Social Responsiveness Scale (SRS; Constantino & Gruber, 2005). They may also choose to use some criterion-referenced assessments such as the Brigance Inventory of Early Development II (IED II; Brigance, 2004), the Assessment of Basic Language and Learning Skills-Revised (ABLLS-R; Partington, 2007), and the Verbal Behavior Milestones Assessment and Placement Program (VB-MAPP; Sundberg, 2008).

Although formal assessments such as the ones listed above can provide valuable information about the strengths and needs of children, developing specific ABA interventions for implementation in the natural environment requires further informal assessments to ensure the goals selected for intervention are developmentally appropriate, meaningful, based on caregiver priorities, and context specific. There are five main purposes of informal assessment when planning such interventions:

1. To determine the child's strengths and interests

2. To determine the child's present levels of performance in communication, social interaction, independent play skills, daily living skills, and/or cognitive skills

3. To determine what, if any, challenging behaviors are occurring and the functions of those challenging behaviors

4. To assess the caregiver priorities for each domain assessed

5. To assess the child's participation in everyday routines

Methods used to gather this information include interviews with primary caregivers, direct observations and interactions with the child, functional behavior assessment, and ecological assessment. These assessments should be completed through a collaborative process involving caregivers and professionals. Typically, the professional who leads the assessment process when planning ABA interventions in the natural environment is a behavior analyst or a special educator with a background in behavior analysis. Other professional team members may include speech-language pathologists, occupational therapists, and medical professionals when appropriate. Depending on the child's age and whether the ABA interventions are provided through an early intervention program, a school district, or through an independent service provider, the child may have an individualized family service plan (IFSP), an individualized education plan (IEP), or an ABA intervention program without an IFSP or IEP. If there is an IFSP or IEP team, the assessment procedures discussed in this chapter can be used for setting IFSP or IEP goals.

ASSESSING STRENGTHS AND INTERESTS

The assessment process should begin with an evaluation of the strengths and interests of the child. There are many reasons for preparing an evaluation at the outset of the process. First, it sets the framework for using a strengths-based approach to early intervention. Many times professionals and parents begin by discussing the child's limitations. While this may seem natural when discussing a child with ASD or any other disability, it does not serve a meaningful purpose. Instead, the conversations should begin with a discussion of what the child does well and what motivates the child.

When we are familiar with the child's strengths and interests, we can then plan interventions that build on those strengths and interests. For example, if we learn that the child already knows all of her letters and is interested in books, we can build on those strengths and interests by teaching more advanced literacy skills and by focusing on enhancing participation in shared book reading activities.

We know that children with ASD have a restricted range of interests. Thus, it is very useful to assess the child's interests so that we can expand on them. For example, if a child has a passion for Thomas the Tank Engine™, that interest can be expanded by exposing the child to books, movies, and toys that include Thomas to build interests in those things even if eventually they do not include Thomas. Another way to use an interest in Thomas is to expose the child to real trains or to other forms of transportation.

We also want to utilize the child's strengths and interests to increase active participation in everyday routines and to enhance learning and development. For example, if the caregiver wants to increase active participation during bathtime and we know the child has strengths with letter identification, foam letters can be placed in the tub. This creates an opportunity to engage in back-and-forth interactions by having the child locate and give specific letters to a sibling or the caregiver.

Another way to utilize the child's strengths and interests is to tap into them when addressing challenging behaviors. Consider a child who loves music. This child has a tantrum every time her mother attempts to put her in her car seat. Prior to putting the child in her car seat, her mother can let her choose a favorite song. Then the mother can have the song playing in the car when she puts the child in the car seat. This may ease the child's anxiety and prevent a tantrum from occurring. Of course, there is no guarantee that simply embedding strengths and interests into undesirable activities will prevent tantrums or other challenging behaviors. However, there is a possibility that doing so can reduce challenging behaviors. Even if more complex behavioral interventions need to be used, you would still want to utilize the child's strengths and interests as much as possible.

Interviews

Figure 3.1 shows an assessment form (with Andrew's results) that can be used when interviewing primary caregivers to determine a child's strengths and interests. Before beginning the interview, be sure to tell the caregiver that you are going to assess his or her child's strengths and interests so that they can be utilized when planning interventions. When using the form, first ask the caregiver to tell you about the child's strengths and interests, and record the information provided. Then use the additional probing questions provided to obtain more information and details. It is not always necessary to ask every question on the form. Choose the ones that will give you new information beyond what was discovered through the introductory question. There may be situations in which the caregiver begins to discuss the child's limitations as opposed to strengths and interests. If that happens, quickly redirect the caregiver by saying something such as, "I will find out about your child's present abilities and challenges later, but right now let's focus solely on the strengths and interests of your child." While the assessment focuses on strengths and interests, there is a question related to aversions and fears. The purpose of that question is to learn whether there are certain things the child finds aversive, frightening, or uncomfortable. The team eventually may choose to address those aversions or fears in order to reduce or eliminate them, but at the outset the team should be aware of them when planning interventions. For example, if the team finds out that a child hates having people sing to her, it would be counterproductive to suggest working on motor imitation while singing songs.

Preference Assessments

The child's strengths and interests can also be determined using preference assessments. Preference assessments help identify potentially reinforcing items, activities, or contexts by having the child make selections between two or more alternatives (Layer, Hanley, Heal, & Tiger, 2008). For example, if the goal is to determine what snacks a child prefers, systematically offer choices and document what the child selects. For example, offer popcorn or chocolate and indicate the selection. If the child selects popcorn, then offer popcorn or crackers and indicate the selection. It is best to do this type of assessment over the course of several days to accurately determine the true preferences of the child. Depending on the child's ability to make choices, the method for presenting options may need to be altered. If the child can point when shown two items, require the child to do so. However, if the child does not yet know how to make choices by pointing, simply have two items available within reach and indicate which one the child selects. Do the same thing with play preferences by presenting choices of toys such as puzzles, toy cars, blocks, or balls. The same process can be conducted for physical activity preferences. Choices may include activities such as jumping on a trampoline, swinging, swimming, playing in a sprinkler, sliding, or climbing. Of course, preferences will change over time so these assessments should be conducted again if the child seems to be developing different preferences. Figure 3.2 provides a sample recording form for conducting preference assessments.

Assessing Strengths and Interests: Caregiver Interview

(page 1 of 2)

Date	Child's name	Interviewer	Caregiver responding
1/5	Andrew	Debra Leach	Jennifer (Mother)

Opening statement	Caregiver response
Tell me about your child's strengths and interests.	He enjoys playing with toys and physical activity.

Additional probing questions	Caregiver response
What makes your child happy?	Going to the playground, playing chase, getting attention, playing hiding games
How does your child prefer to spend his or her time?	Plays for a while and then jumps on the couch or runs around
What are your child's favorite toys or activities?	Puzzles, blocks, shape sorting, train set, mega blocks, bubbles, singing songs ("Wheels on the Bus"; "Heads, Shoulders, Knees, and Toes"), playing with his sister in her princess house, stacking cups
In what areas does your child excel?	Problem solving
What about your child makes you proud?	He is very smart and can figure out how to get what he wants

(continued)

Figure 3.1. Sample Assessing Strengths and Interests: Caregiver Interview. A blank version of this form can be found in Appendix G.

Figure 3.1. *(continued)*

Assessing Strengths and Interests: Caregiver Interview *(continued)*   *(page 2 of 2)*

Additional probing questions	Caregiver response
Who does your child like to spend time with?	Mom, sister, Dad
What are your child's favorite times of the day?	Morning after he gets up, going out, after dinner, bath time, and before bed
What keeps your child's attention?	Spends a bit of time sitting with his puzzles, blocks, and anything you can stack
What are your child's favorite places?	Playground
What would your child never want to give up?	
What are your child's favorite snacks, meals, and drinks?	Teddy Grahams, juice, water, yogurt
Assessing aversions and fears	**Caregiver response**
Does your child have any intense aversions or fears?	No

Preference Assessment Recording Form

Child's name: _____

Date/activity	Choice 1	Choice 2	Selection

Figure 3.2. Preference Assessment Recording Form.

ASSESSING PRESENT LEVELS OF PERFORMANCE

After determining the child's strengths and interests, the next step is to assess the child's present levels of performance in communication skills, social interaction skills, independent play skills, daily living skills, and/or cognitive skills. It is necessary to conduct assessments only for the domains that will be targeted during intervention. Some caregivers choose to address all domains, while others select only one or two domains. It may be easier for caregivers to start with one domain at a time and gradually add more domains once they get comfortable implementing interventions within everyday routines.

Present levels of performance include the child's current abilities in each area as far as what he or she can do independently, with minimal assistance, or with extensive support. It is not necessary to identify all of the skills the child does *not* display. Instead, determine what the child can currently do independently and with support to assist in determining priorities and setting goals. Gather information about present levels of performance through caregiver interviews and direct observations and interactions with the child. It is best to begin by conducting interviews with the caregiver(s), then directly observe and interact with the child in the natural environment to uncover additional information that was not gathered during the interviews. For example, sometimes when you ask the caregiver whether the child displays a certain skill, the caregiver will say, "I'm not sure" or "I think so." In those instances, directly observe and interact with the child to assess those skills. Even if a caregiver is able to answer questions about the child's skills, it may be necessary to directly observe and interact with the child to assess whether the child can display a certain skill across different settings and contexts. Direct observations and interactions can also simply confirm what was learned during the caregiver interview.

Interview portions are always best conducted face-to-face; however, sometimes that is not feasible due to time constraints and responsibilities to supervise the children. It can be very stressful for caregivers to try to have a lengthy conversation while their children need their attention. Therefore, it may work well to e-mail the caregivers the assessment forms and give them approximately one week to complete them. When the forms are returned, follow up with a phone call to clarify any responses if necessary. This way, when the face-to-face meeting takes place with the child and caregivers, direct observations can be conducted without having to spend a great deal of time talking to the caregivers about the child's present levels of performance.

Communication Skills

Numerous skills can be part of a communication assessment. Most people think of communication as verbal language, but much more than speech is involved when evaluating a child's present levels of performance in communication skills (Rogers & Dawson, 2010). It is important to determine the child's ability to use verbal communication and nonverbal communication such as gestures, eye contact, facial expressions, and body language. The child's expressive language skills and receptive language skills (using language and understanding language) must also be considered. This means that when teams are assessing communication skills to plan ABA interventions in the natural environment, they should consider a broad range of functional skills such as the child's ability to express wants and needs, follow directions, gain attention, request help, share enjoyment, share emotions, answer and ask questions, respond to and initiate comments, engage in conversations, and initiate social interactions.

There are formal assessment tools that speech language pathologists may use to gather information about the child's present levels of performance in communication. Useful tools for informal assessment also can be found in the following books: *Early Start Denver Model for Young Children with Autism: Promoting Language, Learning, and Engagement* (Rogers & Dawson, 2010); *The SCERTS® Model: A Comprehensive Educational Approach for Children with Autism Spectrum Disorders* (Prizant, Wetherby, Rubin, Laurent, & Rydell, 2006); *Do-Watch-Listen-Say: Social and Communication Intervention for Children with Autism* (Quill, 2000). Figure 3.3 provides a sample informal assessment tool showing Andrew's present levels of performance in communication. Notice that there is a column for recording information gathered through interviews and another for information gathered through direct observation. Since Andrew was nonverbal at the time of the initial assessment, the questions related to verbal skills were not addressed.

Social Interaction

Although all communication skills require the use of social interaction skills, it is important to assess some additional social interaction skills when planning ABA interventions. Social interaction skills can be thought of in two ways: 1) Skills required for individuals to develop meaningful relationships with others; 2) Specific skills children need to learn to avoid social failure and rejection. Because children with ASD have impairments in joint attention and social reciprocity (see Chapter 1), social interaction impairments arise. Thus, it is crucial to address joint attention and social reciprocity skills at the onset of early intervention with intensity and consistency. Figure 3.4 shows Andrew's results on an assessment tool for determining a child's present levels of joint attention and social reciprocity skills. Like the communication assessment, this tool includes a column to record information gathered through interviews and a column to record information gathered through direct observation.

In addition to assessing joint attention and social reciprocity skills, it is important to assess the child's present levels of performance with specific social skills that influence social acceptance. Figure 3.5 shows Andrew's results on a social skills assessment tool for this purpose. The tool uses a level of independence rating system. This means that for each skill, the assessor indicates whether the child requires maximum prompting, moderate prompting, minimal prompting, or is able to perform the skill independently.

For additional informal assessment tools, see the books referenced earlier for communication assessments. Additionally, the book *Building Social Relationships: A*

Assessing Communication Skills   *(page 1 of 2)*

Child's name: __Andrew_____   Caregiver interviewed: __Jennifer (mother)__   Date: ____1/5_____

Question	Information gathered from interview(s)	Information gathered from direct observation
How does your child express wants and needs? (e.g. grabbing, pulling, pushing, crying/whining, pointing, reaching, eye contact, facial expressions, sounds, words)	Grabbing, pulling, pushing, whining, reaching, eye contact, sounds. If he is hungry and sees me making a meal, he gets in his chair. If his sister has something he wants, he'll try to take it from her. If she does not give it to him, he'll start whining. Many times, he will wait until she is not looking and take it. If he sees bubbles on the counter, he'll try to reach them. He will lift his arms up if he wants to be picked up.	Grabbing, crying
How does your child express frustration or anger? (e.g. crying, hitting, spitting, walking away, eye contact, sounds, words)	Crying. If his sister is the source of frustration he'll push her. Never see him hit.	Crying, task avoidance
What does your child do to gain your attention? (e.g. cry, whine, reach for you, climb on you, make sounds, say words, make eye contact, use facial expressions)	Climbs on me, cries, whines	
What types of directions can your child follow? (e.g. one-step simple, one-step complex, two-step simple, two-step complex, multistep)	One-step simple, maybe two-step simple	Andrew required prompting to follow most simple one-step directions during play activities. He follows directions much better when they are part of a naturally occurring routine.
What sounds does your child babble, if any?	Da , ga, ba, sha, aaaaa, mmm, eeeee	

Figure 3.3.   Sample Assessing Communication Skills. A blank version of this form can be found in Appendix G.

Assessing Communication Skills *(continued)*   *(page 2 of 2)*

Question	Information gathered from interview(s)	Information gathered from direct observation
Describe your child's ability to imitate verbalizations. (e.g. sounds, words, phrases, sentences)	Imitates a sound we make when we play tickle games	Unable to imitate sounds or words during the assessment
What items can your child identify receptively by pointing, touching, giving, or getting, if any? (with books, objects, flash cards, puzzle pieces, etc.)	None	None
How does your child indicate when he doesn't want something? (e.g. shake head, move away, cry, say no)	Moves away, pushes it away, shakes head sometimes	Crying or moving away
How does your child respond to the question, "Do you want _____?" (e.g. take the item, move away, cry, nod head, shake head, say yes/no)	Takes it. If given a choice of two, he'll get the one he wants.	Grabbing
How does your child let you know that something is enjoyable? (e.g. smiling, pointing, nodding, showing, eye contact, sounds, words)	If he is enjoying something, he will smile and look at me.	Smiling and eye contact
How does your child communicate to initiate social interactions with peers? (e.g. eye contact, facial expressions, body language, proximity, gestures, sounds, words)	Sometimes he watches what other kids are doing.	

Assessing Social Interaction Skills   *(page 1 of 2)*

Child's name: _____ Andrew _____ Caregiver interviewed: _Jennifer (mother)_ Date: __1/5__

Describe your child's ability to...	Information gathered from interviews	Information gathered from direct observation
Allow others to join play 1. *Allow an adult or peer to engage in parallel play during a preferred activity* 2. *Allow two or more peers to engage in parallel play during a preferred activity*	Lets me play alongside, but I usually try to play with him. He does not seem to have a problem with that. For example, when he is playing with puzzles, I come and start playing with the puzzles too. He lets me play.	During the assessment, Andrew did allow his mom to join his play, but when I joined his play, he cried.
Respond to joint attention bids from others 1. *Respond to a point with a verbal request to look* 2. *Respond to a verbal request to look* 3. *Respond to a nonverbal play initiation* 4. *Respond to a verbal play initiation* 5. *Give a turn at the request of a peer or adult*	He only turns and looks at me if I say his name. I'd say 90% of the time. I'm not sure he would look at me if I just said "Look."	Andrew did not respond when asked to look with a point. When I said things such as, "Andrew, do you want to do this puzzle with me?" he did not respond. He gave a turn during play activities with maximum prompting.
Maintain joint attention across a variety of activities 1. *Imitate the actions of others* 2. *Respond to requests or directions during ongoing activities* 3. *Respond to questions during ongoing activities* 4. *Respond to comments during ongoing activities* 5. *Make requests or give directions during ongoing activities*	Andrew can engage in back-and-forth interactions for a couple of play activities (e.g. stacking, chase). If I tell him he needs his diaper changed, he'll run. He knows he is going to be chased around. He likes me to chase him around the island in the kitchen. After his bath, he goes into his bedroom and he'll peek out making a sound. And then we play peek-a-boo.	When playing with his mom, Andrew was able to follow some simple directions (e.g. Put the ball on top). When playing with toys with his mom, he typically played with one toy for approximately 1-2 minutes. Andrew required maximum prompting to imitate the actions of others during play.

Figure 3.4. Sample Assessing Social Interaction Skills. A blank version of this form can be found in Appendix G.

Describe your child's ability to...	Information gathered from interviews	Information gathered from direct observation
6. Make comments during ongoing activities 7. Ask questions during ongoing activities 8. Offer toys or materials to a peer or adult during ongoing activities 9. Maintain joint attention for a specified period of time 10. Engage in long chains of reciprocal interactions for a specified period of time		
Initiate joint attention 1. Imitate a peer or adult during play activities 2. Ask for a turn and remain in close proximity while taking a turn 3. Point to something and make eye contact to share information/enjoyment 4. Make a comment to share information/enjoyment 5. Ask a question about something in the environment 6. Initiate play by joining an ongoing play activity with peers 7. Initiate play with a verbal request	He brings me toys. When he plays with his roller coaster toy, he gives me the balls to push down the roller coaster. If his sister starts running around, he will often go after her. When his dad or I come home, he will run to us and give us a hug.	When playing with his mom, he did look up and smile at her a couple of times. During the assessment, I had his sister play with toys in close proximity to him using the same materials he had to assess if he would imitate her. He required maximum prompting to imitate his sister.

Systematic Approach to Teaching Social Interaction Skills to Children and Adolescents with Autism Spectrum Disorders and other Social Difficulties (Bellini, 2006) provides a social interaction assessment tool.

Independent Play Skills

It is important to assess independent play skills to determine the extent to which children are able to play independently and appropriately. Many factors influence a child's ability to play independently, such as attending skills, fine and gross motor

Assessing Social Skills

Child's name: _____Andrew_____ Caregiver interviewed: __Jennifer (mother)__ Date: __1/5__

Skill	Independent	Minimal prompting	Moderate prompting	Maximum prompting
Shares materials during parallel play		X		
Shares materials during joint play			X	
Responds when others offer a turn			X	
Offers a turn to others				X
Maintains attention while waiting for a turn				X
Offers help to others				X
Accepts help from others	X			
Empathizes with the feelings of others			X	
Uses appropriate voice volume	X			
Uses appropriate space with a social partner	X			
Responds to greetings				X
Initiates greetings				X
Uses appropriate eye contact when interacting with others			X	
Gives compliments to others				X
Receives compliments positively	X			
Responds appropriately to facial expressions of others			X	
Responds appropriately to body language of others			X	
Appropriately responds when others are in the way				X
Other:				
Other:				
Other:				
Other:				

Figure 3.5. Sample Assessing Social Skills. A blank version of this form can be found in Appendix G.

skills, cognitive skills, interest and motivation levels, and emotional regulation. To assess independent play skills, you will need to determine the variety of different play activities the child can engage in without support, the length of time the child can engage in independent play, and whether the child engages in appropriate play during independent play activities. Some children can play independently for long periods of time but with only one or two toys or by engaging in stereotypic behaviors. Other children can engage with a variety of toys independently but only for very brief periods of time. Figure 3.6 provides an assessment tool for gathering information about a child's independent play skills, showing Andrew's results.

Daily Living Skills

Daily living skills are additional skills to assess when planning ABA interventions. Often children and adults with disabilities depend on others for their everyday care-taking needs. To increase self-determination skills at an early age, it is crucial to promote independence with daily living skills such as brushing teeth, bathing, washing hands, brushing hair, feeding, drinking, dressing, and toileting. Caregivers may not always promote their child's independence for these skills at young ages. Thus, assessment results may simply show lack of opportunity as opposed to lack of ability. Figure 3.7 shows Andrew's results on an assessment tool for evaluating daily living skills. Like the social skills assessment, it uses a level of independence rating scale.

Cognitive Skills

Another domain that can be assessed when planning ABA interventions is the cognitive domain. This is the domain with which caregivers are most familiar and the one where they feel most comfortable providing intervention for their children. Examples of skills in the cognitive domain include problem solving, vocabulary skills, literacy skills, and math skills. Figure 3.8 provides an informal assessment tool that can be used to assess cognitive skills. The skills included in the assessment include skills for toddlers and preschoolers up to a kindergarten level. A cognitive assessment was not conducted during Andrew's assessment because he was nonverbal, only 23 months old at the time, and had no means of communicating what he knew through expressive communication. However, at age 2½, after seven months of ABA intervention, he certainly could have been assessed for cognitive functioning if the caregivers wanted to address that domain.

ASSESSING CHALLENGING BEHAVIORS

To determine if challenging behaviors need to be assessed, first ask the caregiver if the child displays any challenging behaviors. If the caregiver indicates that challenging behaviors are an issue, then an assessment should be conducted. When assessing challenging behaviors of young children, assess what challenging behaviors are occurring, but more importantly, assess to determine the function or purpose of the challenging behaviors. Understanding the function of the behavior is crucial because once the

Assessing Independent Play Skills

Child's name: _____Andrew_____ Caregiver interviewed: _Jennifer (mother)_ Date: __1/5__

Question	Caregiver response	Direct observation
1. List all of the different activities your child engages in during independent play.	Puzzles, jumping on the couch, running around, shape sorting, trains, blocks, stacking cups	Trains, shape sorting, running around
2. Approximately how long does your child engage in independent play without needing adult support?	Sometimes he can play independently for approximately fifteen minutes. But if he gets frustrated, he will often scream and need my help.	During the assessment, Andrew played independently with the toys his mother listed for approximately one-minute intervals without needing support.
3. Describe any stereotypic or inappropriate behaviors your child engages in during independent play.	When he runs around, he seems to be getting some visual stimulation by watching his feet. He often runs in circles.	Andrew often engaged in repetitive play (e.g. played with the trains in exactly the same manner during the entire interval)

Figure 3.6. Sample Assessing Independent Play Skills. A blank version of this form can be found in Appendix G.

Assessing Daily Living Skills

Child's name: _____Andrew_____ Caregiver interviewed: _Jennifer (mother)_ Date: ___1/5___

Skill	Independent	Minimal prompting	Moderate prompting	Maximum prompting	No opportunity
Eats finger foods	X				
Eats using a fork				X	
Eats using a spoon			X		
Drinks with a straw	X				
Drinks from a cup	X				
Washes hands			X		
Washes face			X		
Brushes teeth				X	
Brushes hair				X	
Uses the toilet					X
Washes body					X
Washes hair					X
Gets dressed				X	
Gets undressed			X		
Other: Dries off after a bath	X				
Other: Gets in his booster seat to eat	X				
Other: Gets in the car	X				

Figure 3.7.   Sample Assessing Daily Living Skills. A blank version of this form can be found in Appendix G.

Assessing Cognitive Skills

(page 1 of 5)

Child's name: _____ Caregiver interviewed: _____ Date: _____

Problem-solving skills	Mastery	Near mastery	Developing	Has not been introduced	Notes
Uses a shape sorter					
Stacks rings					
Nests cups					
Completes peg puzzles					
Completes 24-piece puzzles					
Creates structures with blocks or other manipulative toys					
Matches (objects, shapes, colors)					
Sorts objects, colors, shapes					

Vocabulary	Mastery	Near mastery	Developing	Has not been introduced	Notes
Receptive identification of common objects (3D/2D; field of 2, 3, many)					
Expressive identification of common objects (3D/2D)					
Receptive identification of body parts					

Figure 3.8. Assessing Cognitive Skills. A blank version of this form can be found in Appendix G.

Vocabulary *(continued)*	Mastery	Near mastery	Developing	Has not been introduced	Notes
Expressive identification of body parts					
Receptive identification of verbs (field of 2, 3, many)					
Expressive identification of verbs					
Receptive color identification (field of 2, 3, many)					
Expressive color identification					
Receptive shape identification (field of 2, 3, many)					
Expressive shape identification					

Literacy skills	Mastery	Near mastery	Developing	Has not been introduced	Notes
Recites the alphabet					
Matches letters (uppercase, lowercase, uppercase and lowercase)					
Receptive identification of uppercase letters (field of 2, 3, many)					

(continued)

Figure 3.8. *(continued)*

Assessing Cognitive Skills *(continued)*

Literacy skills *(continued)*	Mastery	Near mastery	Developing	Has not been introduced	Notes
Expressive identi-fication of upper-case letters					
Receptive identifi-cation of lowercase letters (field of 2, 3, many)					
Expressive identifi-cation of lowercase letters					
"Reads" a book independently by turning the pages one at a time from the beginning to the end, holding the book right side up					
Demonstrates concept of print by tracking words with a pointer finger from left to right					
Attends while being read to					
Responds to ques-tions/comments about pictures in a book					
Narrates a story by looking at the pictures					
"Reads" by using memory to recite the story					

Literacy skills *(continued)*	Mastery	Near mastery	Developing	Has not been introduced	Notes
Predicts what a book will be about by looking at the cover and/or hearing the title					
Retells a story					
Responds to literal questions about a story (during and after the story)					
Responds to inferential questions about a story (during and after the story)					
Reads fluently (pre-primer/primer levels)					

Math skills	Mastery	Near mastery	Developing	Has not been introduced	Notes
Rote counts to 10					
Rote counts to 20					
Matches numbers					
Receptive identification of numbers 0–10 (field of 2, 3, many)					
Expressive identification of numbers 0–10					

(continued)

Figure 3.8. *(continued)*

Assessing Cognitive Skills *(continued)*

Math skills (continued)	Mastery	Near mastery	Developing	Has not been introduced	Notes
Receptive identification of numbers 11–20 (field of 2, 3, many)					
Expressive identification of numbers 11–20					
One-to-one correspondence up to 10					
One-to-one correspondence up to 20					
Matches sets of objects to a number (objects and pictures)					
Identifies more and less					
Identifies all, some, and none					
Puts numbers in sequential order					
Adds 1D + 1D with manipulatives					

function is known, appropriate replacement behaviors can be taught that serve the same function as the challenging behavior. All challenging behaviors occur for a reason. While it may seem like the behaviors occur "for no reason at all," that is simply not true. Typically, when a caregiver indicates that challenging behaviors occur for no reason at all, it means that the behaviors occur frequently and may occur for multiple reasons.

Young children with ASD and other disabilities may display challenging behaviors for a variety of reasons. If they lack appropriate verbal and nonverbal communication skills, they may display challenging behaviors to get what they want or to avoid or escape from what they do not want. If they lack social interaction skills, they may display challenging behaviors to manage the anxiety they feel during social situations. Children with ASD often feel fear and anxiety and may display challenging behaviors to channel those fears due to difficulties with emotional regulation. For example, if a child with ASD has a need for sameness and gets fearful and anxious when a parent takes a new route when driving home from the grocery store, the child may engage in challenging behaviors. Challenging behaviors may also be caused by physical pain or discomfort. If a child has a stomachache but cannot effectively communicate that to a caregiver, challenging behaviors may be the result. For children with ASD, some stereotypic behaviors are considered challenging behaviors by their caregivers. Examples of these behaviors may include vocal stims such as shouting out certain sounds, words, phrases, or scripts, visual stims such as staring at certain things that are visually appealing to the child, physical stims such as running around in circles, sensory stims such as smelling the hair of other people, and the list can go on and on. The key is to understand that these behaviors serve a purpose for the children, which can be self-stimulation or emotional regulation.

As was mentioned earlier, in some cases challenging behaviors may serve multiple functions for the child. For example, a child may cry for purposes of avoiding taking a bath, communicating hunger, and regulating fear of new environments. Also, a child may display a variety of different challenging behaviors that serve the same function. For example, a child may scream, hit, or run away to avoid taking a bath due to sensory discomfort.

To effectively determine the function of a challenging behavior, it is often necessary to do a functional behavior assessment (FBA). This typically entails beginning with a functional behavior assessment interview with the caregiver(s). The purpose of the interview is to determine when and where the behavior is most/least likely to occur, with whom the behavior is most/least likely to occur, what typically happens right before and right after the behavior, and what the caregiver thinks the function of the behavior may be. After interviewing the caregiver(s), the assessor would conduct some direct observations using scatter plots and ABC data collection to confirm information gathered during the interview and to gather additional information. Scatter plots show when and where the behavior is most likely and least likely to occur. ABC data examines the antecedents (A) of the behavior (B) and the consequences (C) of the behavior. In other words, the observer examines what happens immediately before the behavior occurs and immediately following the behavior to gain information about the function of the behavior. Finally, all of the data are triangulated to form a hypothesis about the function of the behavior. It is ideal to go a step further and do a functional behavior analysis and actually test the hypothesis by manipulating variables in the environment. However, in such cases a professional with extensive training in ABA should be the person conducting the analysis.

Once the hypothesis for the function of the challenging behavior is determined (and possibly confirmed through a functional behavior analysis), a behavior intervention plan (BIP) is then developed. The BIP includes replacement behaviors that serve the same function as the challenging behavior, along with strategies to teach the replacement behaviors. Also included in the BIP are any environmental changes that need to be made (e.g., reduce noise, create a visual schedule, clearly define play spaces) and any changes to the behaviors of others (e.g., caregivers refrain from positively reinforcing the challenging behavior, siblings provide positive reinforcement for appropriate behavior, peers initiate play with the child). To learn more about the FBA process, visit the Center for Effective and Collaborative Practice web site at http://cecp.air.org/. For information specific to FBA for young children with disabilities, visit the Center on the Social and Emotional Foundations for Early Learning web site at http://csefel.vanderbilt.edu/index.html. Figure 3.9 provides a tool for assessing challenging behaviors and identifying the functions they serve. You can use this tool to record information gathered from an FBA or you can use it without doing a full FBA to gather general information for purposes of setting behavioral goals for ABA interventions. At the time of Andrew's initial assessment, challenging behaviors were not an issue, and thus the behavioral assessment was not conducted.

ASSESSING CAREGIVER PRIORITIES

After assessing the child's present levels of performance, ask the caregivers to identify their priorities for each domain assessed. To do this, first summarize the child's present abilities in each domain. When you are summarizing the child's present abilities, do not list all the skills the child does not have, because that does not lead to setting goals that are developmentally appropriate. Instead, highlight what the child can do independently and what the child can do with support. Below is an example of a summary of Andrew's present level of performance in communication:

> Andrew typically communicates his wants and needs by grabbing, pulling, pushing, whining, reaching, making eye contact, or uttering sounds. He can point to make requests with maximum prompting. He does gesture to be picked up by lifting his arms up. If he gets frustrated, Andrew will communicate his frustration by crying. To gain attention from his parents, Andrew will cry, whine, or climb onto their laps. Andrew can follow one-step simple directions that are presented frequently during naturally occurring routines. He requires moderate to maximum prompting to follow one-step directions that are unfamiliar. When Andrew babbles, he produces the following sounds: "da," "ga," "ba," "sha," "aaaaa," "mmm," and "eeeee." Sometimes he is able to imitate sounds during tickle games. To communicate that he doesn't want something, Andrew will move away, push something away, cry, or sometimes shake his head. When asked if he wants something, if it is present, he will take it. If he is given a choice of two, he will take the one that he wants. He will point to the item with maximum prompting. When he engages in joyful activities, Andrew will sometimes make eye contact with another person and smile. When other children are playing in his proximity, Andrew will sometimes watch what they are doing. He requires maximum assistance to join the play of other children.

After providing a summary of the child's present abilities in a particular domain, say something such as, "Based on what your child is currently able to do, what would you like to see your child learn next?" When you assess caregiver priorities in this way, it guides them to select specific priorities that are developmentally appropriate for their child. Figure 3.10 provides an assessment tool for gathering the caregiver priorities for each domain assessed. Caregivers can indicate up to three priorities for each domain, but it is not necessary for them to provide that many. If the caregivers share many priorities, it is best to have them prioritize their priorities. Do this by

Assessment of Challenging Behaviors

Child's name: _____ Caregiver interviewed: _____ Date: _____

List the challenging behaviors that your child displays.	
Which behavior(s) listed would you like to target for intervention?	

For each behavior that the caregivers would like to target for intervention, complete the information below:

Question	Caregiver response
1. When, where, and with whom is the behavior most or least likely to occur?	
2. What typically happens right before and right after the behavior?	
3. What purpose do you think the behavior serves for your child?	
4. What may be an appropriate replacement behavior that can serve the same purpose?	
5. What changes may need to be made within the environment to decrease the occurrence of the challenging behavior?	
6. How might the behavior of others (e.g. caregivers, siblings, peers) need to be changed to decrease the occurrence of the challenging behavior?	

Figure 3.9. Assessment of Challenging Behaviors.

having them pick their top five priorities overall. Figure 3.10 shows the priorities that Andrew's mother shared. Chapter 4 will discuss how to use the present levels of performance assessment information, the assessment of challenging behaviors, and the assessment of parent priorities to set goals for ABA interventions.

ASSESSMENT OF EVERYDAY ROUTINES

Once the present levels of performance are determined for the domains that will be addressed during ABA interventions, the next step is to assess the child's participation in everyday routines. As was stated in Chapter 1, young children learn best when actively engaged in everyday routines. This also holds true for young children with ASD and other disabilities. However, intensive behavioral interventions often are needed within the routines to increase the child's active participation. When assessing the child's participation in everyday routines, the first step is to ask the caregivers to list the routines in which the child currently participates across home, school, and community contexts. Before having caregivers list the child's everyday routines, explain that the purpose of identifying routines is so they can be examined and utilized for intervention purposes. Table 3.1 shows some examples of routines.

Next, the caregivers select routines they would like to target for intervention. During the routines-based interview process developed by Robin McWilliam (2010), caregivers are asked to give a satisfaction rating for each routine. This can help to determine which routines may require intervention to address challenging behaviors and which ones can be utilized for intervention purposes due to the positive nature of the routine and potential learning opportunities. The assessment tool provided in this book (see Figure 3.11) has a place to list the child's everyday routines and a rat-

Table 3.1.   Examples of routines and activities

Home	School	Community
Caretaking routines (e.g. eating, bathing, dressing, grooming, toileting, bedtime)	Arrival and dismissal routines	Outings for play and entertainment (e.g. park, playground, beach, pool, movie theater, library)
Constructive play activities (e.g. blocks, Legos)	Circle time	Running errands (e.g. grocery store, shopping mall, post office, bank)
Puzzles and shape sorters	Centers	Home visits with friends and family members
Physical play activities (e.g. trampoline, swing, chase, Hide and Seek)	Snack/lunch	Outings in the neighborhood (e.g. bike rides, walks)
Music activities (e.g. singing songs, playing instruments, dancing)	Recess	Participation in extracurricular activities (e.g. dance, karate, gym, swimming)
Cognitive activities (e.g. counting, reading books, letter and number activities)	Small group instruction	Riding in the car

Assessing Caregiver Priorities

Child's name: _____Andrew_____ Caregiver interviewed: _Jennifer (mother)_ Date: __1/5__

Domain	Caregiver priorities
Communication	1. I want Andrew to learn to speak. 2. I want Andrew to be able to tell us what he wants. 3. I want Andrew to be able to ask for help without screaming.
Social interaction/social skills	1. I want Andrew to play more interactively with family members and other kids. 2. 3.
Independent play skills	1. N/A 2. 3.
Daily living skills	1. I want Andrew to be able to feed himself with a spoon. 2. 3.
Cognition	1. N/A 2. 3.
Challenging behavior	1. N/A 2. 3.

Figure 3.10.   Sample Assessing Caregiver Priorities. A blank version of this form can be found in Appendix G.

Assessment of Everyday Routines and Activities

Child's name: _____Andrew_____ Caregiver interviewed: _Jennifer (mother)_ Date: ___1/5___

> 1: The child enjoys the routine and is actively engaged with others.
>
> 2: The child is calm and content during the routine but not actively engaged with others.
>
> 3: The child engages in mildly challenging behaviors during the routine.
>
> 4: The child engages in severely challenging behaviors during the routine.
>
> Circle the routines and activities that you would like to target for intervention.

Home		School		Community	
Waking up routine	2			Gymboree	2
(Eating meals and snacks)	2			Playground	2
(Bathtime)	2			Riding in the car	2
(Playing with toys)	2			Going to friends' houses	2
Playing chase	1				
Playing in the backyard	2				
Playing Hide and Seek					

Figure 3.11. Sample Assessment of Everyday Routines and Activities. A blank version of this form can be found in Appendix G.

ing for each routine. The ratings are designed to indicate the child's emotional state, engagement with others, and any challenging behaviors. This allows the early intervention provider to determine which routines are motivating for the child and thus offer excellent opportunities for teaching new skills, which routines can be targeted to increase engagement with others and to teach new skills that are not currently being tapped into, and which routines may be causing problems within the family that can be improved with behavioral interventions. Once the routines are listed, the caregivers should select the ones they would like to target for intervention. Caregivers may choose to select only one routine to target for intervention purposes initially and then gradually add more as they gain comfort and confidence with implementing interventions within their everyday routines. Figure 3.11 shows the results of Andrew's everyday routines assessment. The school column is left blank because he was not yet attending school at the time of the assessment.

When a routine or activity is selected for intervention, an ecological assessment should be conducted. Ecological assessments provide information about how the environment may influence a child's performance and help to identify skills that are needed within certain contexts (Haney & Cavallaro, 1996). There are many ways to conduct ecological assessments. One method is to use a task analysis approach by determining all of the skills needed for a certain routine or activity within the natural environment and then assessing the skills that the child does and does not have so that goals can be established for increasing the child's participation within that specific context (Browder, 1987). McWilliam recommends assessing routines by determining what the caregivers do during the routine, what the child does during the routine, and what strengths and needs the child has within the routine (2010). This book provides an ecological assessment tool that uses the following procedures:

Step 1.   Ask the caregivers to describe the routine, explaining how the child participates as well as what others do during the routine.

Step 2.   Ask additional probing questions and/or conduct direct observations to assess the child's communication skills, social interaction skills, independence, cognitive skills, and challenging behaviors within the routine.

Step 3.   Ask the caregiver to identify possible next steps for increasing the child's active engagement during the routine, including ways to increase the child's communication skills, social interaction skills, independence, cognitive skills, and positive behaviors. The early intervention provider can offer additional suggestions after the caregiver has had an opportunity to respond.

When going through the three steps above, use the form from Figure 3.12 to record the information gathered. Figure 3.12 shows a sample ecological assessment for the bathtime routine for Andrew.

Ecological Assessment
for Everyday Routines

(page 1 of 2)

Child's name: _____Andrew_____   Routine: _____Bathtime_____ Date: ___1/5___

Opening statement	Caregiver response and/or information gathered from direct observation
Describe what the routine looks like. (Consider how your child participates and the behaviors of others involved in the routine.)	After dinner, I say, "It's bathtime." Andrew goes upstairs. He gets to the bathroom door first and slams the door. I knock on the door. Andrew holds the door so I can't come in, making it a silly game. Eventually he lets me in. I start running the bath water. Then I undress Andrew. I say, "Hands up," and he puts his hands up so I can take off his shirt. Then I undress him the rest of the way. Then Andrew goes in the tub with his sister, and they play and laugh together. They like to play with the vegetable toys in the tub and the strainer. Andrew likes to catch the water that comes out of the strainer. I wash Andrew. When his sister gets out, Andrew puts all of the toy vegetables in the bowl to clean up, and gives me all of the cups they were playing with. He waits to be told to pull the plug to drain the water, and then he does it. Before coming out, he hides behind the glass to play another silly game with me. Then he puts his arms up so I can take him out.

Probing questions	Caregiver response and/ or information gathered from direct observation	Possible next steps
Describe how your child communicates during the routine.	He follows some simple directions. He puts his arms up to indicate that he wants me to get him out of the tub.	He can imitate sounds during the routine. Andrew can work on sharing by having his sister ask him for certain things.

Figure 3.12. Sample Ecological Assessment for Everyday Routines. A blank version of this form can be found in Appendix G.

Ecological Assessment for Everyday Routines *(continued)*   *(page 2 of 2)*

Probing questions	Caregiver response and/ or information gathered from direct observation	Possible next steps
Describe how your child socially interacts during the routine.	He looks at his sister and laughs. He doesn't mind when she plays with the toys with him.	Andrew can learn to imitate his sister throughout the bath routine. Andrew can participate in singing songs with gestures during the routine.
Describe how your child participates independently during the routine.	He laughs a lot and plays with the toys in the tub. He pulls the drain by himself. He can pour the water by himself into the strainer. He cleans up by himself.	He can learn to take his clothes off by himself. He can learn to wash himself.
Describe cognitive skills your child demonstrates during the routine.	(no response)	He can learn to identify body parts.
Does your child engage in any challenging behaviors during the routine?	No.	N/A

CHAPTER SUMMARY

This chapter has provided many assessment tools. The first step should be to assess the child's strengths and interests. Next, assessments are conducted to determine the child's present levels of performance in communication, social interaction, independent play skills, daily living skills, and/or cognitive skills. If challenging behaviors are an issue, the function of those challenging behaviors will be assessed. It is not necessary to assess all domains. Only the domains that will be targeted for intervention need to be assessed. After each domain is assessed, it is important to assess the caregiver priorities to determine what they would like their child to learn next based on what the child can currently do. The next part of the assessment is to assess the child's everyday routines to identify those that will be targeted for intervention. Once routines are selected, ecological assessments are conducted to determine the child's level of engagement, independence, and social interaction during each routine and to determine what new skills the child may need to learn to increase participation. These new skills should be linked to the caregiver priorities that were determined for each domain assessed. In Chapter 4, you will learn how to set goals for increasing the child's active participation in the routines that were selected for intervention. Goals can focus on increasing engagement, independence, and social interaction and will address any of the skills identified in the domains of social interaction, communication, independent play skills, daily living skills, cognitive skills, or challenging behaviors. Chapter 5 includes procedures for designing ABA interventions to address the goals that have been set. Chapter 6 provides data collection tools for monitoring progress. Chapter 7 provides recommendations for collaborating among caregivers and professionals to ensure successful implementation of the interventions.

Goal Setting for ABA Interventions in the Natural Environment

. . . .

This chapter includes procedures for working collaboratively as a team to set goals for ABA interventions in the natural environment using information obtained from the assessments discussed in Chapter 3. Domain-specific goals must be observable, measurable, developmentally appropriate, and functional; they must include criteria for mastery; and they should be positively stated. Examples of goals for each domain are given. Methods for using routines-based ecological assessments to set goals for routines that will be targeted during intervention are included. A matrix for using Activity Based Instruction to plan ABA interventions during everyday routines is provided to help teams support caregivers in systematically planning which goals will be addressed during which naturally occurring routines.

COLLABORATIVE GOAL SETTING

The assessment process described in Chapter 3 leads early intervention teams into a collaborative goal setting process. Just as caregivers and a variety of professionals are involved in the assessment process, the team also provides input when selecting goals for ABA interventions in the natural environment. The individual who led the assessment process will then lead the process of selecting goals by reviewing the child's present levels of performance for the domains being addressed during intervention, the priorities that were indicated by the caregiver, and the information that was obtained related to the child's present levels of participation in everyday routines.

Goals for IFSPs or IEPs are typically written annually with the intention that the child will master the goal within a year. Goals for ABA interventions, however, should be much more short-term. As a general rule, goals set for ABA interventions should be mastered within three months or less. ABA is designed to make meaningful changes in the life of the individual using systematic instruction to bring about changes fairly quickly. Broad skills are broken down to allow teams to target very discrete skills the child needs to communicate, interact socially, learn, and increase independence. Data are collected frequently and progress is monitored consistently to continually make instructional decisions. If the goals selected are likely to be achieved within three months or less, the data should show improvement within weeks of intervention, if not sooner. Often, in order to teach the skills needed for the child to master an annual IFSP or IEP goal, the goal needs to be broken down into short-term goals even if the short-term goals are not included in the IFSP or IEP. These short-term goals can certainly be part of ABA interventions in the natural environment.

CRITERIA FOR WRITING GOALS

Goals for ABA interventions in the natural environment must be observable, measurable, developmentally appropriate, and functional. In addition, goals should indicate criteria for mastery and be positively stated. Each of these requirements is discussed in detail in the sections that follow.

Observable

A goal is observable if we can actually see the child demonstrating the skill. This is directly linked to the *behavioral* dimension of ABA. A goal such as "Abby will enjoy playing with her sister" is not observable because we cannot always see enjoyment. Enjoyment is not a particular behavior, and it often looks quite different for different individuals, especially if you consider some children with ASD who may not show positive affect much of the time. Instead, a goal can state "Abby will play alongside her sister during indoor and outdoor play activities and make eye contact with her sister and smile at least once during each play activity." Caregivers and interventionists can then observe whether the child is engaging in those play behaviors with her sister. Not only must we be able to see what the goal is stating, the goal must be written in such a way that a variety of individuals will look for exactly the same behaviors. The first example about Abby enjoying playing with her sister would probably result in different individuals looking for different behaviors; however, the second example about Abby playing alongside her sister during indoor and outdoor play activities making eye contact and smiling at least once during each play activity lets all individuals know exactly what to look for.

Measurable

A goal is measurable if we can measure what we see the child doing. There should be something in the goal statement that indicates the type of measurement system that will be used. Considering Abby's goal discussed in the previous section, her performance can be measured by indicating the types of indoor and outdoor activities she engages in while playing alongside her sister and by indicating whether or not she makes eye contact and smiles at least once during each play activity. The goal should not be written in a way that leaves methods for measuring performance open to interpretation. For example, if Abby's goal states "Abby will play alongside her sister during indoor and outdoor play activities and share enjoyment while playing," various individuals may measure "sharing enjoyment" differently. However, if the goal states "Abby will play alongside her sister during indoor and outdoor play activities and make eye contact with her sister and smile at least once during each play activity" it is clear that the occurrence of eye contact and smiling at least once during each activity is what is being measured.

Developmentally Appropriate

As was discussed in Chapter 1, developmentally appropriate practice (DAP) entails setting goals that are challenging and achievable (NAEYC, 2012). To identify developmentally appropriate goals, assessments such as the ones discussed in Chapter 3 must first be conducted to identify the child's present ability levels. Then, meaningful goals can be set that are challenging and achievable by examining what the child can already do and what would be the next steps developmentally. This is related to the *applied* dimension of ABA (Baer, Wolf, & Risley, 1968). In order for a goal to be meaningful for the child, it has to be achievable. Frequently goals are selected from a developmental scope and sequence checklist or from a commercially developed curriculum. Sometimes the goals selected are not developmentally appropriate because the child does not have the skills required to achieve the goal. For example, a goal may be for the child to initiate greetings. However, if the child does not yet respond to greetings from others, it would be more developmentally appropriate to teach that skill first. Once the child can respond to greetings, it will be much easier to teach the child to initiate greetings.

Sometimes goals are not developmentally appropriate not because of a lack of prerequisite skills but because the child is not yet ready to learn the skill indicated. The author-provided scenario below shows an example of a situation in which a child simply was not ready to learn a skill that was being targeted:

> Back in the early days of implementing discrete trial training, I remember spending months working on teaching a 2-year-old boy with autism, Austin, to differentiate between girls and boys receptively. This meant I would hold up a picture of a girl and a picture of a boy and say, "Where's the boy?" or "Where's the girl?" For months, the data showed 50% accuracy, give or take. I tried using figurines instead of pictures and even real children, but no matter what, Austin could not learn the skill. Finally, my supervisor agreed to remove the goal from Austin's discrete trial program since progress was not being made after trying several different teaching methods. I continued to work with Austin and his family for years to come. When he was 5 or 6 years old, one day I asked his mom, "By the way, did Austin ever learn to differentiate between boys and girls?" Her reply was, "Yes, he has no problem with that now. We never even taught him. He learned incidentally as he developed."

To set goals that are developmentally appropriate, use assessment data related to the child's present level of performance, as was discussed in Chapter 3. When you are summarizing present levels of performance by highlighting what the child currently can do independently and what the child can do with support, it will be easy to see the logical next steps in the child's development. Those logical next steps should be targeted for goal selection. For example, Abby's goal related to playing alongside her sister and making eye contact and smiling would not be developmentally appropriate if she currently engages in challenging behaviors every time her sister enters her play area. If that were the case, a more developmentally appropriate goal would be "Abby will allow her sister to join her play in a positive manner by remaining in the play area and staying calm." Once Abby is able to tolerate her sister playing in close proximity to her, then it would be developmentally appropriate to teach Abby how to make eye contact and smile at her sister during play to share enjoyment.

Functional

If a goal is functional, it is meaningful for the child and will make a positive impact on the child's life when achieved. This is also directly related to the *applied* dimension of ABA (Baer, Wolf, & Risley, 1968). If goals are clinical in nature, they may not be very meaningful for children. For example, a goal that states, "Alex will match three-dimensional objects to pictures" is probably not a functional goal for many children. A good way to determine whether a goal is functional is to ask the "so what?" question. If the child masters the goal, so what? How will this new skill improve the child's life? If the question cannot be answered in a meaningful way, it is probably not a functional goal. So, instead of teaching Alex to match objects to pictures, it may be more meaningful to teach him to receptively identify common objects in the natural environment, in pictures, and in videos. So what? If he can learn to identify common objects by pointing to them, he can use that skill to communicate with others. Alex can then learn to request by pointing to desired objects or pictures of desired objects. Later, this skill can help enhance his participation during social activities and learning activities by enabling him to point to pictures to indicate responses to questions and make comments to others.

Another way to determine whether a goal is functional is to find out if the skill is useful across home, school, and community settings. While some goals will be specific to a certain setting, most goals should be written so that the child learns a new skill that can be applied across a variety of settings and contexts. So, instead of writing a goal that says, "Justin will share materials with peers during small-group speech therapy sessions," you can make it meaningful across home, school, and community contexts by writing, "Justin will share materials with peers during structured and unstructured play activities." Of course, the targeted goal may first be achieved during structured play activities, but eventually, the goal should be expanded to unstructured play activities for generalization purposes.

Criterion for Mastery

Each goal should have a criterion for mastery to allow the team to determine when the child has achieved the goal. One common way to state a criterion for mastery is to indicate a percentage, such as "James will play with peers on the playground 90% of the time." While percentages can be a useful, meaningful way to indicate mastery, it may not always be the most appropriate data collection method. For example, it would be extremely difficult to record the percentage of time James plays with peers on the playground. Theoretically, it could be done by using a stopwatch and watching him like a hawk throughout the play period so you could stop the timer when he is not playing with peers and restart it during the times when he does play with peers. You could then divide the amount of time he played with peers by the total time he spent on the playground. Realistically, this method of data collection would not be feasible for caregivers or intervention providers. Instead, a criterion for mastery may be "James will play with peers on the playground for the majority of the play period." The caregivers can then use an individualized rating system such as the following to estimate the amount of time he played with peers:

1.   Never played with peers

2.   Played with peers for a small portion of the play period

3.   Played with peers for approximately half of the play period

4.   Played with peers for the majority of the play period

Other ways to indicate a criterion for mastery in addition to percentages and individualized rating systems include the use of level of independence ratings, frequency counts, and yes/no data collection. These methods will be discussed in detail in Chapter 6. In addition to indicating a criterion such as a percentage, rating, level of independence, frequency, or yes/no, it is important to indicate the number of days or weeks or in what contexts the child should meet the indicated criterion in order for the goal to be considered mastered. For example, James's goal should be enhanced as follows: "James will play with peers on the playground for the majority of the play period for five consecutive play periods." Adding, "for five consecutive play periods," ensures that the team does not consider the goal mastered after James plays with peers for the majority of the time on the playground on only one occasion.

Learning takes place in four stages: skill acquisition, fluency, maintenance, and generalization. During the skill acquisition stage, children are just beginning to develop a skill. At the fluency stage, the child can demonstrate the skill with ease. At the maintenance stage, the skill is maintained for a long period of time. Finally, at the generalization stage, the child is able to demonstrate the skill across a variety of contexts and settings. Criteria for mastery should, at the very least, ensure that the child has reached the fluency stage, if not maintenance or even generalization. Too often, interventionists consider a goal mastered during the skill acquisition phase instead of continuing intervention until the child is fluent, can maintain the skill over time, and can generalize the use of the skill. When only the first stage of learning is mastered, the child may end up losing the skill because he or she did not move beyond skill acquisition.

Positively Stated

Finally, goals should be positively stated by indicating what new skills the child will learn. Avoid writing behavior reduction goals such as "Sean will refrain from crying

Table 4.1.   Criteria for writing goals for ABA interventions in the natural environment

Criterion	ABA dimension addressed	Description
Observable	Behavioral	The goal is written in such a way that the child can actually be seen demonstrating the skill.
Measurable	Behavioral	The goal is written so that various individuals would measure it in the same manner.
Developmentally appropriate	Applied	The goal is based on the present levels of performance of the child by determining what the child can currently do and selecting goals that are the logical next steps.
Functional	Applied	The goal is meaningful for the child and adequately answers the "So what?" question. Most goals should have meaning across home, school, and community settings.
Criterion for mastery		The goal includes a statement to determine when the child achieves mastery. Specific measurement systems should be indicated.
Positively stated		The goal states the skill the child is expected to learn, not what the child should refrain from doing.

to get what he wants." Instead, state what Sean will do instead of crying: "Sean will point to request desired items." When goals are positively stated, they focus on skill development. When you are tempted to write a goal that is not positively stated, consider what the child can learn to do to avoid engaging in a negative behavior. For example, if the team is tempted to write the goal "Lauren will not have a tantrum when she doesn't get what she wants," they can discuss more appropriate ways that Lauren could deal with not getting what she wants. A positively stated goal may be "When Lauren does not get what she wants, she will remain calm or show mild frustration such as an unhappy facial expression or a very brief period of whining or crying." Table 4.1 summarizes the criteria for writing goals for ABA interventions in the natural environment.

WRITING DOMAIN-SPECIFIC GOALS

For each domain that is assessed, the team will collaboratively set goals based on the caregiver priorities and the child's present levels of performance. When the assessments are done well and valuable information is collected, goal setting should be fairly easy. The team simply has to examine the present level of performance statements and the caregiver priorities, then use professional judgment to write the most meaningful goals for the child. It may be that the team can write 10 different goals for one domain because of the wealth of information that was gathered during the assessment process. However, the caregivers will be responsible for implementing the interventions to address each goal during their everyday routines, so it is not feasible to have them work on 10 or more goals at the onset of intervention. Instead, select one to three goals for each domain to target first.

Select the goals that will make the most positive impact on the child's development. This is where professional judgment comes in. Consider a situation in which possible social goals for a child include sharing toys, maintaining joint play for 5 minutes, and using appropriate voice volume across settings. While all three goals seem meaningful, if professional judgment is going to be used to select just one goal, maintaining joint play is probably the most meaningful goal to start with. If the child learns how to maintain joint play, she or he might naturally begin to share toys while playing without having to be explicitly taught sharing skills. Although voice volume can and should be addressed when appropriate, it is more important to get a child to engage in joint play with others than to work on voice volume. If voice volume continues to be a problem, it can be addressed a little later. In Chapter 3, the following present level of performance for Andrew's communication skills was shared:

> Andrew typically communicates his wants and needs by grabbing, pulling, pushing, whining, reaching, making eye contact, or uttering sounds. He can point to make requests with maximum prompting. He does gesture to be picked up by lifting his arms up. If he gets frustrated, Andrew will communicate his frustration by crying. To gain attention from his parents, Andrew will cry, whine, or climb onto their laps. Andrew can follow one-step simple directions that are presented frequently during naturally occurring routines. He requires moderate to maximum prompting to follow one-step directions that are unfamiliar. When Andrew babbles, he produces the following sounds: "da," "ga," "ba," "sha," "aaaaa," "mmm," and "eeeee." Sometimes he is able to imitate sounds during tickle games. To communicate that he doesn't want something, Andrew will move away, push something away, cry, or sometimes shake his head. When asked if he wants something, if it is present, he will take it. If he is given a choice of two, he will take the one that he wants. He will point to the item with maximum prompting. When engaging in joyful activities, Andrew will sometimes make eye contact with another person and smile. When other children are playing in his proximity, Andrew will sometimes watch what they are doing. He requires maximum assistance to join the play of other children.

Andrew's mother indicated that her priorities in the area of communication were that Andrew would learn how to speak, be able to communicate what he wants, and be able to ask for help in a calm manner. Based on these priorities, the information gathered during the assessment, and professional judgment, the following communication goals were selected for Andrew for the onset of his ABA intervention program:

1. When given a choice of two items, Andrew will request the desired item by pointing and making eye contact independently for 5 consecutive days.

2. Andrew will consistently imitate at least 10 different sounds or words.

3. Andrew will ask for help by giving the toy or object to an adult paired with eye contact while remaining calm independently for 5 consecutive days.

The following social goals were selected for Andrew based on the present level of performance assessments and the caregiver priorities:

1. Andrew will maintain joint play with adults for at least 5 minutes for 5 consecutive days using a variety of different toys.

2. Andrew will imitate a variety of motor movements during play routines independently for 5 consecutive days.

Notice that each communication and social interaction goal is observable, measurable, developmentally appropriate (based on the assessment information), functional, has a criterion for mastery, and is positively stated. Although many different goals could have been written for Andrew based on the present level of performance assessments, the above goals address the caregiver priorities and were deemed the most meaningful for increasing his communication and social interaction skills. Examples of domain-specific goals are provided in Table 4.2.

Table 4.2. Examples of domain-specific goals

Domain	Examples of goals
Communication	1. The child will consistently request at least 10 different desired items by naming the item and either pointing or making eye contact independently.
	2. The child will use pictures to request desired activities, given a field of two, independently for 5 consecutive days.
	3. The child will independently respond to comments related to present activities using at least one-word utterances for 5 consecutive days.
Social interaction	1. The child will allow an adult or peer to engage in parallel play during preferred activities, remaining calm throughout the activity, for 5 consecutive days across several different activities.
	2. The child will give a turn at the request of a peer or adult independently for 5 consecutive days.
	3. The child will respond positively to a verbal play initiation from a peer at least once during each recess period using either a positive verbal response, a positive gesture, or by beginning to play in a positive manner for 5 consecutive days.
Independent play skills	1. The child will play independently with puzzles for at least 5 minutes for 5 consecutive days.
	2. The child will engage in independent "reading" activities for at least 5 minutes independently for 5 consecutive days by turning pages one by one from beginning to end and/or by narrating books based on the pictures or memory from when the book was read aloud.
	3. The child will independently engage in imaginative play by engaging in appropriate, nonrepetitive use of the materials and/or by narrating play for at least 10 minutes using materials such as pretend kitchens, dolls/dollhouses, farms/farm animals, figurines, and dress-up materials for 5 consecutive days.
Daily living skills	1. The child will independently use a spoon to eat foods such as pudding and yogurt for 5 consecutive days.
	2. The child will independently take off socks and shoes for 5 consecutive days.
	3. The child will independently drink from a half-full 4-ounce cup for 5 consecutive days.
Cognitive skills	1. The child will receptively identify basic shapes (circle, square, triangle, and rectangle) in a field of two with 100% accuracy.
	2. The child will expressively identify all uppercase letters of the alphabet with 100% accuracy.
	3. The child will rote count up to 10 with 100% accuracy.
Positive behaviors	1. The child will remain buckled in the car seat while riding in the car 100% of the time.
	2. The child will sit at the table during mealtimes for at least 10 minutes for 5 consecutive days.
	3. At night, the child will stay in bed and fall asleep after being tucked in for 2 consecutive weeks.

USING A ROUTINES MATRIX TO ORGANIZE GOALS

Once domain-specific goals have been selected, an activity-based instructional approach (Pretti-Frontczak & Bricker, 2004) can be used to systematically plan opportunities for embedding ABA instruction related to those goals during naturally occurring routines. Within this framework, the naturally occurring routines and activities are used as opportunities to teach new skills. This method has been shown to be effective in increasing motivation and generalization. To best implement activity-based instruction for ABA interventions, use a matrix to determine which goals will be addressed during which routines. Creating a matrix allows caregivers to view the goals they are currently working on within the context of their day on one sheet of paper. Figure 4.1 shows

ABA Activity-Based Instruction Matrix

Child's name: __Andrew__   Date: _____1/5_____

DIRECTIONS:

1. List the domain-specific goals across the top of the table using an abbreviation for the goal or a number to represent the goal.
2. List the routines selected for ABA interventions down the left side of the table.
3. Put X's in the boxes to indicate which goals will be addressed during which routines. Instead of X's, the initials of the caregiver who will implement the intervention during the specific routine can be indicated if desired. This allows multiple caregivers to share responsibility for implementing the interventions.

	Goal: Choose by pointing, field of two	**Goal:** Imitate sounds and words	**Goal:** Ask for help	**Goal:** Joint play	**Goal:** Motor imitation
Routine: Bathtime	Mom, sister, Dad	Mom, sister, Dad		Mom, sister	Mom, sister
Routine: Eating	Mom, Dad	Mom			
Routine: Playing with toys	Mom, Dad	Mom	Mom	Mom	Mom, Dad
Routine:					
Routine:					

Figure 4.1.   Sample ABA Activity-Based Instruction Matrix. A blank version of this form can be found in Appendix G.

Goals for Targeted Routine

Child's name: _____ Andrew _____ Routine: _____ Bathtime _____ Date: __ 1/5 ___

Domains	Goals
Communication skills	1. When given a choice of two items, Andrew will request the desired item by pointing independently for 5 consecutive days. 2. Andrew will consistently imitate at least 10 different sounds or words.
Social interaction skills	1. Andrew will maintain joint play with adults for at least 5 minutes for 5 consecutive days using a variety of different toys. 2. Andrew will imitate a variety of motor movements during play routines independently for 5 consecutive days.
Independence	1. Andrew will wash himself. 2. Andrew will undress and dress himself.
Cognitive skills	1. Andrew will receptively identify body parts.
Positive behaviors	N/A

Figure 4.2. Sample Goals for Targeted Routine. A blank version of this form can be found in Appendix G.

Andrew's initial ABA interventions on a matrix listing the routines selected for intervention, the domain-specific goals, and goals that will be worked on within each routine throughout the day. Directions for completing the matrix are included on the form. As goals are mastered and new goals are added, the matrix will need to be changed. If a child is receiving ABA interventions in a school setting, it is recommended to create a separate matrix for school. The staff can share responsibility for implementing the interventions throughout the school day by indicating who will work on which goals during which routines.

WRITING GOALS BASED ON ECOLOGICAL ASSESSMENTS OF ROUTINES

As was explained in Chapter 3, the team should not only assess specific domains for purposes of goal setting but also conduct ecological assessments of the child's communication skills, social interaction skills, level of independence, cognitive skills, and challenging behaviors during the everyday routines selected for ABA intervention. These assessments can then be used to set goals specific to the targeted routines. When goals are selected for targeted routines, they should be linked to the domain-specific goals as often as possible to avoid overwhelming caregivers with too many goals that require specific interventions. Figure 4.2 provides a form for writing the goals for a specific routine, with an example of the goals written based on the ecological assessment of Andrew's bathtime routine that was included in Chapter 3 (see Figure 3.12).

CHAPTER SUMMARY

This chapter has provided procedures for using assessment information to set goals for ABA interventions in the natural environment. In summary, all domain-specific goals must be observable, measurable, developmentally appropriate, functional, include criteria for mastery, and should be positively stated. Teams should consider caregiver priorities and the present level of performance statements to set goals and prioritize them by using professional judgment to determine which skills will have the most positive impact on the child's life. Once domain-specific goals have been set, the team then uses ecological assessments (see Chapter 3) to determine which goals will be addressed during the routines selected for intervention. The team will also make suggestions for increasing the child's engagement, independence, and social interaction for each routine selected. The last step in goal setting is to create an activity-based instruction matrix to provide caregivers with a one-page summary showing the goals they will be addressing during the ABA interventions and the routines in which those goals will be addressed. The matrix can even show the intervention responsibilities for different caregivers involved in implementing the ABA interventions. Chapter 5 includes procedures for designing ABA interventions to address the goals selected.

Developing Teaching Procedures for ABA Interventions in the Natural Environment

· ·

Chapters 3 and 4 focused on procedures for assessing and setting goals. Teams can set domain-specific goals as well as goals for selected everyday routines. Once goals have been identified, it is time to develop ABA teaching procedures for each goal that can be implemented in the natural environment. ABA teaching procedures must be *conceptual* (they must utilize teaching strategies that are supported by behavioral research) and *technological* (they must be written and explained in a manner that will allow them to be replicated with fidelity). This chapter begins with an overview of positive behavioral supports and an explanation of their relevance to designing and implementing ABA teaching procedures for young children with ASD and other disabilities in the natural environment. Definitions and examples portray a variety of behavioral teaching strategies that can be used to teach skills across all domains. Specific examples illustrate how the behavioral strategies can be used in conjunction with one another to develop *conceptual* and *technological* teaching procedures to address individual goals.

POSITIVE BEHAVIORAL SUPPORTS

The strategies that will be discussed in this chapter are considered positive behavioral supports because they are preventative, proactive, and supportive. Ethical considerations have led the field of ABA to move away from the use of aversive consequences to change behavior. One of the core principles for behavior analysts is being just. This means treating others the way you would like to be treated (Bailey & Burch, 2011). Thus, when choosing interventions to address challenging behaviors or to teach new skills, early interventionists should choose interventions that are nonaversive to the child to the maximum extent possible.

Some caregivers and teachers feel that punitive consequences must be given to let a child know that a certain behavior is unacceptable. In practice, however, delivering a punitive consequence after a challenging behavior often increases the likelihood that the child will maintain or increase the use of the challenging behavior because the negative attention serves as a positive reinforcer. By contrast, the positive behavioral supports discussed in this chapter are nonaversive, preventative, proactive, and supportive strategies that can be used to teach positive behaviors as well as social interaction skills, communication skills, daily living skills, independent play skills, and cognitive skills while encouraging active participation in everyday routines.

BEHAVIORAL TEACHING STRATEGIES

There is some controversy among educators of young children with autism spectrum disorders when it comes to labeling certain teaching strategies as behaviorally based or developmentally based. Some professionals view themselves as behaviorists and others as developmentalists. Behaviorists focus their work on the use of intervention approaches that utilize principles of ABA such as discrete trial training (Lovaas, 1987), incidental teaching (Hart & Risley, 1975; McGee, Morrier, & Daly, 1999), pivotal response treatment (Koegel et al., 1999), and applied verbal behavior (Sundberg & Michael, 2001). Developmentalists focus their work on the use of intervention approaches such as floor time/DRI (Wielder & Greenspan, 2003), RDI (Gutstein, Burgess, & Montfort, 2007), SCERTS® (Prizant et al., 2006), and the Denver model (Rogers & Dawson, 2010). These different viewpoints often lead to an unfortunate divide among leading researchers and practitioners who share the same commitment to the use of effective interventions for young children with ASD. There is much to be learned from the work of leading researchers from both the behavioral and developmental perspectives, and the strengths from both perspectives can contribute to quality interventions for young children with ASD.

This book is behavioral inasmuch as it focuses on applying the seven dimensions of ABA when assessing, designing, and evaluating interventions for young children with ASD, although many of the strategies discussed in this chapter can be considered more developmental than behavioral. In fact, many strategies that are used as part of behavioral interventions are similar or even identical to strategies used as part of developmental approaches. For example, "following the child's lead" is commonly used in natural behavioral approaches such as IT and PRT, and it is also used in all of the developmental approaches. In behavioral approaches the "shaping" strategy positively reinforces successive approximations of a desired behavior. Although developmental approaches may not name the strategy "shaping," they often use the same approach by gradually increasing expectations for the child and by recognizing even small gains through positive affect and attention.

Even though many strategies are similar across behavioral and developmental approaches, however, there are numerous differences. For example, behavioral approaches have explicit, clearly defined teaching procedures for each skill being taught, while developmental approaches may suggest more global teaching strategies that can be used for a variety of targeted skills. In developmental approaches there is a broad focus on building social relationships through the use of responsive teaching strategies and increased positive affect. This is something that is often lacking in behaviorally based interventions but should certainly be considered. Thus, the strategies shared in this chapter draw from both the behavioral and developmental literature. First, traditional behavioral strategies will be explained, including positive reinforcement, extinction paired with differential positive reinforcement, prompting/fading procedures, shaping, embedded discrete trials, time delay, task analysis, video modeling, self-monitoring, and behavioral momentum. Then additional strategies that come from both behavioral and developmental literature will be shared, including following the child's lead, environmental arrangements, balanced turn taking, modeling/request imitation, contingent imitation, peer-mediated interventions, Social Stories, priming, and augmentative and alternative communication strategies.

Positive Reinforcement

Positive reinforcement entails delivering consequences immediately following a behavior that increase the likelihood that the behavior will occur again in the future. Thus, if caregivers or interventionists indicate that positive reinforcement isn't working, what they are actually saying is that the consequences are not reinforcing for the child. The same types of things may not motivate young children with ASD for long. They may have a strong desire for certain things one week but no interest in those things the following week. When this happens, conducting preference assessments can be quite helpful (see Chapter 3). It is important to understand, however, that there are many different types of positive reinforcement. These include tangible reinforcement, activity reinforcement, token reinforcement, social reinforcement, and natural reinforcement. Table 5.1 provides a definition and examples for each type of reinforcement.

Generally speaking, it is best to use natural and social reinforcers as often as possible when implementing ABA interventions with young children with ASD and other disabilities. There is a misconception that children with ASD often require tangible and activity reinforcement to be motivated to complete tasks and meet expectations. In reality, children with ASD often respond very well to social reinforcement and natural reinforcement. If children are constantly presented with tasks that are difficult and boring, then they will probably require tangible and activity reinforcers. But when children are engaged in meaningful, interesting activities with the necessary supports to achieve success, social and natural reinforcements may be sufficiently motivating. That is why this book focuses on embedding ABA interventions within naturally occurring routines and activities. These everyday routines and activities are often much more motivating than clinical settings and isolated interventions. Just as typically developing children are naturally motivated to learn within everyday routines, young

Table 5.1.   Types of positive reinforcement

Reinforcer type	Definition	Example
Natural reinforcement	The consequence that immediately follows the behavior is what would be considered a natural positive consequence of the behavior.	The child says, "Cookie," and the caregiver gives the child a cookie.
Social reinforcement	The consequence that immediately follows the behavior is a desirable social response from others, such as specific praise, high fives, tickles, or warm facial expressions.	The child stacks a tower of blocks, and the caregiver smiles and says, "Give me five! That is such a tall tower!"
Token reinforcement	The consequence that immediately follows the behaviors is a token that will later be traded in for an activity or tangible reinforcer.	At preschool, the teacher gives the child a happy face sticker each time she responds to questions during circle time. After the child gets five stickers, she gets to choose a special activity.
Activity reinforcement	The consequence that immediately follows the behaviors is access to a favorite activity.	After a child sits at a table and finishes her meal, she is able to have 10 minutes on the computer.
Tangible reinforcement	The consequence that immediately follows the behaviors is a favorite food, drink, toy, or object.	Each time the child counts a set of objects correctly, she gets a small, edible treat.

children with ASD are as well. They may need more support and interventions to be able to effectively and efficiently learn in those contexts, but that certainly doesn't mean they should not have opportunities to learn during naturally occurring routines and activities.

It is very important that caregivers and interventionists do not reinforce escape-motivated behaviors. This means that the child should not be reinforced for doing something by letting the child get away to do something else. If children are reinforced for completing a certain task or engaging in a certain activity by getting away from that very task or activity to do something else, they may learn to do something just to get away from it. When this happens, it's almost like the child becomes a ticking time bomb who is keeping it together just long enough to be able to finish the task or request in order to quickly dash away to something much less interactive. It becomes quite difficult to build internal motivation when external reinforcers are the main focus for the child. Thus, the key is to make everyday routines and activities naturally reinforcing by accessing children's strengths and interests and then increasing their active engagement, independence, and opportunities for successful social interactions throughout their participation in their daily routines.

Many times caregivers and intervention providers do not use enough positive reinforcement. If a child has ASD or any other disability, she needs to be told about all of the things that she is doing well as often as possible. Frequently children with special needs are directed and redirected by adults and told what they are doing wrong

either verbally or nonverbally throughout the day. When children need intensive intervention and continually require direction and redirection, it is important to shower
them with as much natural and social reinforcement as possible to keep them motivated and feeling good about themselves.

Differential Reinforcement of Alternative Behavior

As was stated at the beginning of this chapter, the strategies presented in this book are
considered positive behavioral supports because they are preventative, proactive, and
supportive. Thus, punishment procedures are not included as suggested interventions
for young children with ASD and other disabilities. With that said, caregivers must
know how to deal with challenging behaviors that arise. One of the most effective
ways to decrease a problem behavior is to place the problem behavior on extinction
and positively reinforce a behavior that is more desirable. This is called differential reinforcement of alternative behavior, or DRA (Vollmer & Iwata, 1992). The extinction
procedure entails ignoring the problem behavior. This means not giving any attention
to the child, positive or negative, when the problem behavior occurs. No reprimands
are delivered, no threats are given, no negative facial expressions are displayed, no
physical consequences are administered, and no techniques are used to try to calm
the child down or verbally reason with the child. The purpose of using extinction is
to take away consequences that are maintaining or increasing the problem behavior.
However, extinction alone may not eliminate the problem behavior without positively
reinforcing a more desirable behavior at the same time. This means that in addition to
ignoring the problem behavior, the caregiver positively reinforces the child for a positive behavior the child displays instead of the problem behavior. Here is an example
of using DRA:

> The problem behavior for a young child with ASD, named Samantha, consists of screaming when
> she wants to be picked up. To decrease this problem behavior, her parents use extinction by re-
> fraining from picking her up when she screams. They completely ignore the screaming. When
> Samantha stops screaming, her mother or father says something such as, "Do you want me to pick
> you up?" and they pick her up. Samantha's parents consistently follow this procedure. They also
> look for ways to reinforce Samantha by picking her up when she displays positive behaviors or less
> problematic behaviors. For example, Samantha typically screams to be picked up when someone
> new comes in the house. Her parents prevent the screaming by positively reinforcing Samantha by
> picking her up when she runs to them instead of waiting for her to start screaming. Samantha also
> screams to be picked up when she is tired. Before she screams, she usually rubs her eyes. So, her
> parents begin to offer to pick her up when they see her rubbing her eyes instead of waiting for her
> to scream. Each time her parents offer to pick her up when she isn't screaming, they also work on
> teaching her to say "Up." Soon Samantha learns that screaming will not result in getting picked
> up. She learns that in order to be picked up she can either be in close proximity to her parents
> while remaining calm or she can say, "Up."

When using DRA, it is often necessary to teach the more desirable behavior, or
replacement skills, if the child doesn't already have the skills required to engage in the
more desirable behavior. To effectively teach replacement skills, however, caregivers
must be able to implement a variety of effective teaching procedures such as the strategies discussed throughout the rest of this chapter.

Prompting/Fading Procedure

The prompting/fading procedure consists of teaching skills and behaviors by providing prompts or cues but then fading out the intensity of the prompts as soon as possible to promote independent responding. Children with ASD often get "blamed" for being prompt dependent, or reliant on certain cues or assistance in order to respond to certain requests or to make initiations. The truth is that if a child is dependent on prompts, intervention providers and caregivers are more likely to blame than the child. If adults do not systematically fade out the prompts they are giving, then children will certainly become reliant on those prompts. For example, if the caregiver says, "What do you want?" every time the child whines, the child may become prompt dependent and only make a verbal request after hearing, "What do you want?" Therefore, that verbal prompt needs to be faded out so the child can initiate a request without the need for a prompt.

Two different methods can be used to fade prompts systematically: least-to-most prompts and most-to-least prompts (Wolery & Gast, 1984). With least-to-most prompts, each time a request is made, the least intrusive prompt is used that will likely result in a positive response from the child. However, if the child does not respond with the prompt provided, the intensity of the prompts is increased to enable the child to respond successfully. For successive opportunities, the intensity of the initial prompt is lessened until the child responds without any prompts at all. For example, if a mother wanted to use least-to-most prompts to teach her child to verbally request desired items instead of whining, the mother can begin with a minimally intrusive prompt such as putting her hands out and shrugging with a look of question on her face as if to say, "What do you want?" without actually saying anything. If the child doesn't respond, the mother can increase the intensity of the prompt by saying, "What?" If there is still no response, the mother can say, "What do you want?" For the next successive opportunity, the mother should use a prompt that is a little less intrusive than the one that was needed to get the child to respond the time before.

When using most-to-least prompts, begin with intensive prompting to ensure success and then lessen the intensity of the initial prompts. The same example used for least-to-most prompts can also be used to demonstrate using most-to-least prompts, but it would look like this: The mother would start with an intrusive prompt such as saying "What do you want?" when the child whines. Then at the next opportunity, the mother will say "What?" instead of "What do you want?" At the next opportunity, the mother will put her hands out and shrug with a look of question on her face as if to say, "What do you want?" without actually saying anything. After that, the mother will just raise her eyebrows in question, and so on until the child will initiate verbal requests independently.

Whether you are using most-to-least prompting or least-to-most prompting, the key is planning successive opportunities. Prompts cannot be systematically faded if learning opportunities are spread too far apart. When teaching a new skill, it is important to have many repeated opportunities so the prompts can be faded out as quickly as possible. Another point to consider is that with some children prompts can be faded with each new learning opportunity, but with other children it may take longer to be able to fade prompts. The children may require several opportunities to perform with a certain level of prompting before fading out the prompts.

How do you decide between least-to-most and most-to-least prompting? Generally, if the child does not have any of the skills required to respond to a certain request, most-to-least prompting is used to prevent frustration and task avoidance. However, if the child has some but not all of the skills required, you can use least-to-most prompting to promote independent responding as quickly as possible and prevent prompt-dependency.

Prompts can be physical, gestural, auditory, and visual (Wolery, Ault, & Doyle, 1992). Physical prompts entail some sort of touch. This can range from hand-over-hand assistance to a light tap to encourage a child to respond. It is best to avoid using hand-over-hand assistance whenever possible, however. When you provide hand-over-hand assistance, you are basically telling the child that she cannot do what you are asking her to do. This often results in children becoming like marionette puppets and letting the adults do with them what they want instead of actually learning the new skill. Ways to give physical assistance without using hand-over-hand prompts include providing gentle physical guidance and gradually removing your light touch and physical support until the child is responding independently. Examples of verbal prompts include repeating directions, giving verbal reminders, or providing verbal redirection. Visual prompts may include objects, pictures, picture symbols, or written words. Gestural prompts may include pointing, nodding or shaking your head, holding up a certain number of fingers to refer to something, or using a gestural symbol such as holding up a hand to indicate "stop." Some may say that physical prompts are the most intensive followed by verbal, visual, and then gestural. However, that is not necessarily true. Consider teaching a child to build with blocks independently. A physical prompt such as lightly touching the child's hand to encourage her to pick up a block may actually be less intensive than a verbal prompt such as saying "Get a block." So the type of prompt used is not as important as whether the prompts are systematically faded out until the child no longer requires them.

Shaping

The shaping strategy entails positively reinforcing successive approximations of a desired behavior (Cooper, Heron, & Heward, 2007). In other words, use the shaping strategy by setting a desired outcome or goal and then positively reinforcing the child as she or he gets closer and closer to meeting the expectation. This requires caregivers to understand that in order for a child to get from point A to point Z, the child must first go through B, C, D, and so on. When children are reinforced as they make small improvements, they are more likely to be motivated to meet the next expectation. Using the shaping procedure allows caregivers to set small goals so that children can easily learn the required skills, which helps to reduce anxiety and increase motivation.

Below is a scenario that describes a father, Jim, using the shaping strategy to teach his son, Michael, to initiate a request for juice by saying "juice."

> When Jim decided to use shaping to teach Michael how to initiate a request for juice by saying, "Juice," Michael was requesting juice by crying and waiting for Jim to say, "Do you want juice?" So, at the onset of the intervention Jim decided to positively reinforce Michael by giving him a sip of juice when he pointed to his juice cup even if he was crying while he did so. Once Michael could point to his juice cup, Jim only positively reinforced him with the juice if he pointed without crying. After Michael could point to request juice without crying, Jim only provided positive reinforcement if Michael pointed and imitated the word "juice." Once Jim could point and imitate the word "juice," Jim positively reinforced Michael when he said "juice" independently (without needing a model to imitate). The goal set was for Michael to initiate a request for juice by saying "juice," and Jim helped Michael achieve that goal by using shaping.

Embedded Discrete Trials

Chapter 2 gave a brief overview of discrete trial training (DTT) (Lovaas, 1987). Although the use of DTT in clinical settings may result in limited generalization and lack of motivation, the teaching sequence used in DTT can certainly be applied within naturally occurring contexts. When the discrete trial teaching sequence is applied in natural contexts, it is referred to as embedded discrete trials (McBride & Schwartz, 2003). The teaching sequence is as follows:

1. Antecedent (request, direction, comment, question, or other opportunity to respond)

2. Prompt (used if necessary, but faded out as soon as possible)

3. Behavior (the desired response from the child)

4. Consequence (positive reinforcement)

This teaching sequence can be used to teach many skills throughout a child's day. For example, if one of the goals for a child is to respond to comments, embedded discrete trials can be used during routines such as play activities, meals, bathtime, driving in the car, book sharing activities, and a variety of school-based routines. Below is an example of a mother using an embedded discrete trial during a book sharing activity with her daughter, Emily.

Antecedent: Mom makes a comment about the book she is sharing with Emily by saying, "The boy does not look happy."

Prompt: Emily doesn't respond to the comment, so Mom repeats the comment again and points to the boy's face.

Behavior: Emily says, "He's crying."

Consequence: Mom replies, "Yes, Emily! The boy is crying. He is very sad." She gives Emily a little tickle.

Embedding discrete trials repeatedly within routines throughout the child's day is essential. Children must have multiple learning opportunities, or trials, for the most efficient learning to occur. In many cases, children need some mass trialing at the initial stages of learning a new skill. This means that the caregiver would present 3 to 10 embedded discrete trials, one right after another. Once the child begins to respond without a great deal of prompting, the trials can then be distributed over the course of the child's day. However, when distributing trials throughout the day, caregivers should plan to use at least 10 to 20 embedded discrete trials for each goal.

Time Delay

There are two approaches to using the time delay strategy. One approach entails delivering a prompt immediately following an antecedent (request, direction, comment, question, or other opportunity to respond) to ensure that the child delivers a successful response. After several trials like this, the prompt is slightly delayed (by approximately 2 seconds) to see whether the child will respond without the prompt. If the child doesn't respond after the slight time delay, the prompt is delivered to ensure a successful response. Each time the antecedent is delivered, the length of the time delay is slightly increased until the child can respond without the prompt (Snell & Gast, 1981).

The second method for using time delay does not necessarily require an increase in the length of time delay with each new antecedent, but each antecedent is given with a short period of wait time accompanied by an expectant look and/or expectant body language (Halle, Marshall, & Spradlin, 1979). An expectant look can be a smile, raised eyebrows, or a warm facial expression. Expectant body language can include leaning in toward the student, shrugging shoulders, or putting hands up as if to say, "What?" It is important to be in close proximity to the child and at eye level when using time delay so the child learns to interpret the expectant looks and body language as "invitations" for a response or initiation. When caregivers use time delay, it should be done in a positive, supportive manner to encourage the child to respond without fear of getting the answer wrong. This type of time delay strategy generally is not used as much as it could be when working with young children with ASD and other disabilities. Caregivers are often quick to begin prompting if the child doesn't respond or initiate immediately. This can cause children to become dependent on these prompts. To avoid prompt-dependency, caregivers can use time delay before prompting to allow opportunities for the children to respond without assistance. Of course, if the child doesn't display an appropriate response after time delay is used, caregivers can then use other strategies to ensure success. Below is an example of a preschool teacher using time delay to encourage a child, Jeremy, to respond to a question during the morning circle time:

> During morning circle, the teacher engages the children in calendar activities. One of the activities that the teacher thinks Jeremy can actively participate in is telling about the weather outside, since weather is one of Jeremy's special interests. During the morning circle, however, the early intervention service provider observed that Jeremy did not reply when the teacher asked him about the weather outside. The teacher then said, "Let's see if someone can help you," and called on another student. It was suggested that when the teacher asks Jeremy about the weather she first calls Jeremy up to the calendar so that she and Jeremy can be in close proximity and face-to-face. Then after she asks Jeremy about the weather, she should use a brief time delay paired with an expectant look

and expectant body language to encourage him to respond. If he doesn't respond within about 5 seconds, the teacher should provide a prompt such as pointing to the picture that describes the weather outside so Jeremy can respond successfully. When the teacher tried using this time delay strategy the next day, Jeremy did require a prompt; however, each day after that throughout the week he was able to respond with just a brief time delay. The following week, Jeremy was able to respond to the teacher's question without any time delay at all.

Task Analysis/Chaining

The task analysis/chaining strategy involves breaking down an individual task into sequential steps and teaching the child the task in a stepwise fashion (Spooner, 1984). There are three ways to use chaining: forward chaining, backward chaining, and total task presentation. Forward chaining involves teaching the first step, then the second, then the third, and so on until the child can complete the entire task independently. Backward chaining involves teaching the last step, the second-to-last step, and so on until the child can complete the entire task independently. Total task presentation involves gradually increasing the child's participation by involving the child in more and more steps of the task with each new opportunity, but not necessarily starting with the first or last step. Instead the child is involved in the steps that are the easiest for the child to do first.

Whether you use forward chaining, backward chaining, or total task presentation depends on the task being taught and the individual child. For example, you may use forward chaining to teach a child how to eat yogurt with a spoon because each step of the task is at the same level of difficulty for the child. But you may use backward chaining to teach the child to wash hands because the easiest part is drying hands with a towel. You may use total task presentation to teach a child to go up and down the slide at the playground because the easiest step is to slide down once the child is sitting on the top. With each new opportunity the child can learn more and more steps involved in getting to the top of the slide, sliding down, and going back to the stairs to go back up. Task analysis/chaining can be used to teach daily living skills, independent play skills, positive behaviors, social skills, communication skills, and cognitive skills.

Video Modeling/Video Self-Modeling

With the video modeling strategy, children with ASD and other disabilities learn to imitate certain behaviors by watching a video of another child engaging in the desired behavior (Bellini, Akullian, & Hopf, 2007). Interventionists can also use video self-modeling, which involves showing children videos of themselves engaging in a desired behavior to increase the use of that specific behavior (Dowrick, 1999). Some may wonder how you can get a video of a child engaging in behavior that the child is learning. This is done through behind-the-scenes prompting. The individuals capturing the video of the child engaging in the desired behavior may prompt the child a great deal to get the child to demonstrate the desired behavior; however, the prompting is not captured on the video. This way, the children see themselves engaging in the behavior independently, which is the desired result of the intervention. Children with ASD often learn best when visual supports are used. Thus, videos demonstrating desired behaviors can certainly help many children learn expectations.

Digital cameras that have video capability are quite useful for implementing this strategy because caregivers and interventionists can quickly capture a behavior on video and upload it to the computer for children to view. This strategy is particularly appropriate when children with ASD are included in preschool classrooms because there are many positive models to capture on video demonstrating the behaviors teachers want the children to learn. Once the behaviors are caught on video, the children can view them, talk about what they observed, role-play what they observed, and then receive reinforcement for demonstrating those behaviors in the natural context of the classroom. A variety of positive behaviors and social, communication, cognitive, daily living, and independent play skills can be taught through video modeling or video self-modeling.

Self-Monitoring

Self-monitoring involves teaching children how to monitor their own performance to increase motivation and promote positive behaviors. This strategy has been widely used to improve academics, social behaviors, and independent functioning of individuals with ASD (Coyle & Cole, 2004; Dipipi, Jitendra, & Miller, 2001; Koegel, Koegel, Hurley, & Frea, 1992; Pierce & Schreibman, 1994). When children are involved in recording their own behaviors, they become more aware of their own actions and may be more likely to improve their behaviors than they would be if adults were solely responsible for documenting performance.

Some may think that self-monitoring should be used only with children in upper elementary, middle, or high school settings. However, there are many ways to use self-monitoring with children age 3 and up with ASD and other disabilities. For example, children can be taught to monitor their performance when learning toileting skills, how to initiate play with peers, how to eat a variety of different foods, how to ask for help in a preschool classroom, how to wash independently when taking a bath, and so on. When using self-monitoring with young children with ASD and other disabilities, use the following steps adapted from literature on using self-monitoring in school settings (Ganz, 2008):

1. Select a specific target behavior.

2. Teach the child the behavioral expectations for the target behavior.

3. Have the child select a positive reinforcer.

4. Teach the child how to record performance and self-reinforce using role play activities.

5. Have the child and caregiver both record the child's performance initially, but fade out the caregiver recording once the child is consistently recording accurately.

Self-monitoring is particularly useful in preschool classrooms because it lessens the amount of teacher involvement in managing behaviors and thereby allows the teacher to better meet the needs of all children in the classroom. Figure 5.1 provides an example of a self-monitoring tool used in teaching the child to play with peers during recess instead of engaging in solitary play. The child needs to be informed about the goal (playing with peers during recess) and taught how to play with peers during recess, how to monitor performance using the self-monitoring tool, and how to self-reinforce when appropriate. When using the self-monitoring tool, the child simply draws a circle around the star if he or she played with peers most of the time, a circle around the happy face if the child played with peers some of the time, or

I played with friends during recess!

Date: _____

Figure 5.1. Self-monitoring example.

a circle around the check mark if the child needed help from the teacher to play with peers. Positive reinforcement is noted for each level. The bottom level does not have positive reinforcement associated with it since the goal is for the child to play with peers independently. However, caregivers can certainly decide to have some type of positive reinforcement for all levels. It is not recommended to use sad faces when the child doesn't display the target behavior. When we choose to target a behavior for self-monitoring it is because the nature of the child's disability requires that the child learn specific behaviors that other children may learn incidentally. It is not appropriate to make children feel bad about behaviors they display or do not display that are a result of the disability. It is appropriate, however, to inform the child of the goal being targeted, provide explicit instructions for performing the desired behavior, and align positive reinforcement with specific outcomes.

Behavioral Momentum

Behavioral momentum is a strategy that increases a child's motivation to respond to tasks that are difficult or challenging. It involves making two or three requests that are easy for the child before making a request that is more difficult and then repeating the pattern of easy-easy-difficult when continuing to make requests (Davis et al., 1994; Jung, Sainato, & Davis, 2008; Mace & Belfiore, 1990). Here is why this strategy should be used when planning interventions for children with ASD and other disabilities: When children are continually presented with challenging tasks one after the other, they will typically shut down and stop trying because they do not feel they can be successful. If this is the case, using behavioral momentum can provide the motivation that children need by continually delivering requests that are easy for them and systematically interspersing more challenging requests. For example, if a goal for the child is to expressively identify colors, and the child already knows red and blue, the caregiver can use the following teaching sequence:

1. Hold up something red and ask the child what color it is.

2. Hold up something blue and ask the child what color it is.

3. Hold up something yellow and ask the child what color it is (since this is a more challenging color, the caregiver will likely need to use an embedded discrete trial at this step).

4. Hold up something red and ask the child what color it is.

5. Hold up something blue and ask the child what color it is.

6. Hold up something yellow and ask the child what color it is (use an embedded discrete trial again if necessary).

7. Continue with this sequence of easy-easy-difficult until yellow becomes one of the "easy" colors.

Following the Child's Lead

Following the child's lead is a behavioral strategy that is used to increase communication and social skills. This strategy is one of the essential elements of pivotal response treatment (Koegel et al., 1999) and incidental teaching (McGee, Morrier, & Daly, 1999). It entails beginning an interaction with a child by attending to what the child is doing at the time. To make following the child's lead an effective strategy, caregivers should position themselves face-to-face with the child, present materials, actions, and objects that are interesting to the child, and make requests that are at the child's developmental level (Zanolli, Paden, & Cox, 1997). For example, if a child is playing in the sandbox filling up a dump truck with sand, the caregiver, peer, or interventionist should begin an interaction by joining the child in filling up the dump truck with sand. The adult or peer should get face-to-face with the child and provide opportunities for the child to engage successfully. This might entail asking the child to share the shovel, offering a new sand toy for the child to play with, making a comment, asking a question, giving a direction, or any other interaction that will encourage engagement between the child and a play partner.

It's important for caregivers to understand the value of following the child's lead. The natural instinct of adults when attempting to establish interactions between a child with ASD and a typically developing peer is often the opposite of following the child's lead. They may try to get the child to attend to what the peer is doing instead. When adults do this, they end up fighting three battles at the same time: dealing with the child's social interaction and communication difficulties, dealing with the difficulties that children with ASD often have with shifting their attention, and dealing with the difficulty of engaging children with ASD in activities for which they do not have the interest level or the skill set required.

This does not mean that following the child's lead will automatically result in positive interactions. The child may still try to escape from the interactions. If that happens, be sure to use additional strategies to establish interactions with the child. Do not just follow the child around. That is not the intention of this strategy. Follow the child's lead to increase the likelihood that the child will be able to engage, but then use a combination of other strategies to establish and maintain the interaction when necessary.

Environmental Arrangements

Another effective strategy involves making environmental arrangements that promote communication and interaction (Koegel et al., 1999; McGee, Krantz, & McClannahan, 1985; Skokut, Robinson, Openden, & Jimerson, 2008). Four different environmental arrangement strategies can be used to improve social interaction and communication skills for children with ASD and other disabilities:

1. Place desired or needed items out of reach to provide opportunities for the child to make requests.

2. Give small amounts of desired or needed items to encourage the child to ask for more.

3. Do something unexpected to increase initiations from the child.

4. Reduce environmental stimuli to limit distractions and prevent sensory overload.

Place Desired Items Out of Reach   When placing desired items out of reach, it is important that the items remain visible to the child to encourage the child to ask for the desired item. When children are at the initial stages of learning how to request, placing desired items out of reach might simply mean holding an item in your hand and preventing the child from grabbing it by keeping it out of arm's reach. You can teach the child to request the item by pointing, naming the item, saying "Please," saying "More," or using augmentative communication such as pointing to a picture or using a voice output device. Most-to-least prompting may need to be used in combination with this environmental arrangement to avoid problem behavior while the child is learning a new requesting skill.

Give Small Amounts   Although giving small amounts of something can be a great way to teach a child to ask for more, it is important to treat the child respectfully when you are doing this. Below is an actual incident that occurred during a discrete trial training session that highlights this point:

> A 5-year-old boy was working on learning colors. Each time he successfully responded by pointing to the color stated by the therapist, he would get a small piece of a cookie. After a few consecutive trials, the boy said, "Don't give me crumbs. It's not nice to do to people!"

So, when you are giving small amounts of something to promote communication, try to be considerate. If you are going to use this technique during snack times, for example, don't give ridiculously small amounts. Instead, give less than a full serving so the child can ask for more. For example, you can give the child two small pretzels and encourage the child to ask for more as opposed to giving the child a handful of small pretzels. If the child is at school and engaging in a desirable activity with paint, the teacher can give a small dollop of paint to encourage the child to ask for more.

Do Something Unexpected   Doing something unexpected can facilitate communication and social interaction with some young children, especially children with ASD who like things to be the same or who like things to occur in a certain order. Here is an example of doing something unexpected to facilitate communication and reciprocal interactions with a 2-year-old boy with autism, named Jared:

> Jared's father discovered that when Jared put his shapes in his shape sorter, he put the shapes in using exactly the same order every time. There were 10 shapes in total. The interventionist tapped into Jared's desire to put the shapes in the sorter using a particular order by doing something unexpected: hiding the next shape so Jared would have to ask for it. The interventionist let Jared put in the first three shapes, then took the triangle (the fourth shape in the sequence). Jared began to get anxious, but the interventionist said, "I have the triangle" in a playful tone of voice and showed Jared the triangle. Jared then used language to request the triangle. The interventionist continued with this strategy of doing something unexpected by hiding a shape and then teaching Jared to say, "Where is it?" The interventionist was also able to teach Jared to follow directions by telling Jared where the shape was hidden so he could listen and then find the shape. It was a fun activity that the father could replicate again and use when similar opportunities presented themselves.

Reduce Environmental Stimuli Some children with ASD and other disabilities have difficulty communicating and interacting due to overstimulation. There are times when environments have too much stimuli for the child to process, and consequently the child may shut down and be unable to effectively communicate and interact. Examples of things that may overstimulate a child include high noise levels, fluorescent lighting, odors, large groups of people, a large quantity of materials presented to the child, and excessive visual stimulation. Some kids may require adjustments to stimuli such as these in order to take in the environmental stimuli, process the stimuli, and effectively respond and function in the environment. Here is an example:

> A 3-year-old boy with autism, Jake, attends a community preschool. He loves building with blocks. However, every time he goes to the block center, there are at least three other children on the carpet, the blocks are spread all over the carpet, the other children are all talking, and Jake quickly gets overstimulated. This may result in Jake screaming, knocking down the structures other children are building, or leaving the center. To deal with Jake's sensory overload, the teacher creates another block center for Jake and a peer. The center is at a small table with two chairs and just enough blocks for two children. At first, the teacher facilitates the interactions between Jake and the child who joins him at the table to ensure his success. The teacher is able to fade out support and Jake can engage in the specially designed block center with one peer independently. Gradually, more stimuli are added back into Jakes block center, such as more blocks and an additional peer. Eventually Jake is able to transition to the block center on the carpet as he learns to adjust to more environmental stimuli.

Balanced Turn Taking

Balanced turn taking entails purposefully setting up interactions that enable the child and caregiver to engage in balanced, back-and-forth interactions to increase the duration of attention and engagement (MacDonald & Carroll, 1992). For example, the caregiver may sing the child's favorite song and pause at intervals throughout the song to allow the child to sing the next word or phrase. This back-and-forth interaction is easy to establish if the child likes the song and has the expressive communication skills needed to participate in the back-and-forth singing routine. Other examples of using balanced turn taking include taking turns putting blocks on a tower, putting pieces in a puzzle, hiding when playing Hide and Seek, rolling a ball back and forth, and being the leader in imitation games such as Simon Says.

Stanley Greenspan describes several ways of using balanced turn taking as part of the floor time intervention (Greenspan & Weider, 1998). Although floor time is not an ABA approach, the strategies suggested by Greenspan are useful when setting up balanced turn taking interventions. These strategies include playful obstruction, playful construction, and playful negotiation. The playful obstruction and playful construction strategies are used to turn nonfunctional or noninteractive routines into back-and-forth social interactions. Playful obstruction entails getting in the way or blocking something a child is doing in order to establish an interaction. For example, a caregiver may use playful obstruction when a child is heading toward the back door to go outside. The caregiver can run to the door to get there first and block the doorway. This way the child must communicate with the caregiver to go outside. The caregiver may simply lock the door, get down to the child's eye level, and use time delay to encourage the child to use words or gestures to make a request to open the door or go outside. In this scenario, the caregiver promotes communication by obstructing the child's action of opening the back door and going outside. After the caregiver uses playful obstruction, playful negotiation can then be used to "stretch" the interaction as much as possible without causing extensive frustration to the child. For example, if the caregiver uses playful obstruction as the child goes to the back door and the child says "outside," instead of opening the door at that point and ending the interaction, the caregiver can playfully negotiate to establish longer chains of back-and-forth interactions. The caregiver may ask, "What are you going to do outside?" or make a comment such as "You have no shoes on." When the child responds to the comment or question, the interaction can be continued for as long as possible.

Playful construction is used in a similar fashion, but instead of blocking the child or getting in the way of what the child is doing, the caregiver joins the child when the child is engaging in a noninteractive activity or self-stimulatory activity in order to establish balanced turn taking. For example, if a child is lining up toy cars, the caregiver can join the child and create a road made of blocks to use for the cars. This can set up balanced turn taking by creating a play routine in which the child and caregiver take turns pushing the cars along the road. Once this turn taking routine has been established, the caregiver can use playful negotiation to increase the length of back-and-forth interactions. This can be done by asking the child to get a particular car such as the red car or the police car, the caregiver can stage a car crash and ask the child to help fix the road, or the caregiver can put barriers on the road to encourage the child to communicate to remove the barriers. In using these strategies suggested by Greenspan it is essential that caregivers remain playful. The goal is not to frustrate the child but to stimulate back-and-forth interactions by creating playful obstacles to encourage balanced turn taking.

Modeling/Request Imitation

The modeling/request imitation strategy entails first modeling or showing the child what you expect the child to do, then providing an opportunity for the child to imitate the model and receive immediate feedback (Buffington, Krantz, McClannahan, & Poulson, 1998). The feedback would consist of positive reinforcement if the child imitated the modeled behavior or prompting to enable the child to imitate the behavior. Although prompting may be used if the child does not imitate the modeled behavior, the purpose of using this strategy is to eliminate the need for verbal or physical prompts. Many times caregivers immediately prompt a child to engage in a certain behavior using verbal or physical prompts without first demonstrating what it is they would like the child to do. Many times if the child is shown what to do, she or he can imitate independently without requiring additional prompts. When children can respond independently without prompts, they feel a great sense of participation, accomplishment, and success.

All children learn by imitating others. Although typically developing children automatically imitate just about everything they see, children with ASD and other disabilities may require more explicit instruction (modeling/request imitation) in order to imitate others. Here are some examples of using modeling/request imitation:

1. While giving her child a bath, a mother picks up a toy cow and says, "Moo!" The mother then gives the cow to the child and says, "Your turn!" The child says, "Moo!" Mom smiles at the child and gives the child a tickle on her tummy.

2. During a puzzle activity, a father notices his son having trouble getting a piece to fit. The father takes the piece, puts it in to show the child where it belongs, and gives the piece back so he can imitate the response. The child then puts the piece in just like his father did. The father says, "You put it in!" and smiles.

3. When playing at the playground with her 2-year-old son with autism and her 4-year-old daughter, a mother realizes that her son does not know how to go down the slide. He stands on top but does not slide down. The mother asks her daughter to go first and say, "Watch me!" and slide down. After the daughter slides down, the mother encourages her to look up at her brother and say, "Your turn!" The boy sits and slides down. When he gets to the bottom his sister smiles and gives him a high five.

Contingent Imitation

Contingent imitation is somewhat similar to following the child's lead. This strategy entails imitating what the child is doing to establish an interaction (Cautilli & Dziewolska, 2005; Gazdag & Warren, 2000). Sometimes contingent imitation is the only way to get a child with ASD to attend to another individual if the child is deeply engaged in a certain activity. For example, a child may be engaging in a stereotypic behavior such as opening and closing a door. The caregiver may try to redirect the child but cannot get the child to break away from the activity. Then the caregiver can imitate the child by opening and closing the door for purposes of getting the child to attend to the caregiver instead of the door. While it may sound odd to imitate a stereotypic behavior, the point is to get the child to interact. Once the child responds to the contingent imitation either by looking at the caregiver or making a verbalization or gesture, the caregiver should attempt to redirect the child into a more meaningful interaction. For example, if the child looks at the caregiver after the caregiver imitates opening and closing the door, the caregiver may decide to turn it into a game by getting on the other side of the door and teaching the child to knock on the door and wait for the caregiver to open it and say, "I see you!" Of course, this would require the participation of another person such as another caregiver, a sibling, or an interventionist so that one person can be on one side of the door while the other teaches the child to knock. Using contingent imitation can be very simple, though. A caregiver can simply imitate the child and once the child responds in some way, modeling/request imitation can be used to make the interaction more reciprocal and appropriate.

Peer-Mediated Intervention

Peer-mediated intervention entails teaching typically developing peers how to use strategies to promote interactions with children with ASD. Peers are trained to use behavioral strategies such as the ones discussed in this chapter to promote positive interactions with children with ASD (Morrison, Kamps, Garcia, & Parker, 2001). Unless training and support is provided to typically developing peers, they often refrain from interacting with children with ASD because the children may not respond to their initiations (DiSalvo & Oswald, 2002). However, when peers learn how to get a child with ASD to respond, they are often positively reinforced by the response and increase their initiations with the child (Robertson, Green, Alper, Schloss, & Kohler, 2003). Caregivers can use peer-mediated interventions to improve social interaction skills, communication skills, daily living skills, independent play skills, and cognitive skills; to promote positive behaviors; and to increase participation in everyday routines and activities.

Social Stories

Social Stories (Gray & Garand, 1993) have been used with children with ASD to teach a variety of social skills and positive behaviors. The strategy entails writing a short story that clearly illustrates behavioral expectations. The story is written in the present tense from the child's perspective to allow the child to relate to the information provided in the story. Three types of sentences can be used when writing Social Stories: descriptive, perspective, and directive. Descriptive sentences provide information about the particular setting or situation. Perspective sentences provide information about the thoughts and feelings of other people. Directive sentences provide information about what the child should do in the particular setting or situation. Carol Gray suggests including two to five descriptive sentences for each directive or perspective sentence. The following is an example of a social story used to teach a child with ASD the behavioral expectations for circle time at preschool:

> My name is James. I love going to preschool. In the morning, my teacher asks all of the children to sit on the carpet for circle time. We all have a carpet square to sit on. When my teacher says, "It's time to come to the circle," I walk to my carpet square and sit down. My teacher is so happy when I go to my carpet square and sit down. During circle time, my teacher asks questions, sings songs, and tells stories. Sometimes all of the kids get to participate. Sometimes she will call on one child to answer a question. I participate with all of the kids when the teacher asks us all to do what she says. I stay quiet when another child is answering a question. My teacher gives me a sticker after circle time if I stay on my carpet square, participate with the kids, and stay quiet when other children answer questions. Circle time is so much fun!

Social Stories can be used in conjunction with a variety of other strategies to increase their benefit. Caregivers and teachers can ask children comprehension questions about the stories and engage them in role plays to increase their effectiveness (Chan & O'Reilly, 2008). Video modeling can also be used with Social Stories to enhance learning (Sansosti & Powell-Smith, 2008). It is quite easy to use PowerPoint to create the social story and insert pictures of the child and videos of the child or other children demonstrating the expectations. Prompting/fading procedures and positive reinforcement are effective in teaching children the behaviors targeted in the Social Stories

(Swaggart et al., 1995). Children can also be taught to use self-monitoring strategies to record their own performance related to meeting the expectations set forth in the Social Stories (Thiemann & Goldstein, 2001).

Priming

Priming is a method of supplying information to prepare a child for effective performance of a task or activity (Bainbridge & Smith Myles, 1999). Information can be supplied verbally or through pictures, modeling, video modeling, or written information for children who can read. Priming can be used to teach a new skill or to address a challenging behavior. For example, caregivers may use priming by showing a child how they brush their teeth for several days before expecting the child to brush her own teeth. When dealing with a challenging behavior such as crying when a caregiver doesn't read the exact book the child wants read, prior to beginning the book sharing routine the caregiver can say, "First we will read this book" (show the nonpreferred book), "and then we will read this book" (show the preferred book). Priming can help ease the anxiety of young children with ASD and other disabilities.

Augmentative and Alternative Communication Strategies

Some children with ASD and other disabilities must use augmentative and alternative communication strategies (AAC) to communicate with others. These strategies can be used with children who are nonverbal or have limited verbal expression abilities. Examples of AAC strategies include the use of pictures, symbols, sign language, gestures, and voice output devices. The Picture Exchange Communication System (PECS) is a widely used AAC strategy (Bondy & Frost, 2001). It entails teaching children to use symbols to communicate with others. Many studies have shown that the use of PECS can result in increased vocabulary, increased spontaneous communication, and in some cases, functional verbal speech (Bondy & Frost, 1994; Ganz & Simpson, 2004; Mirenda, 2003; Schwartz, Garfinkle, & Bauer, 1998). With the use of PECS, other picture symbol interventions, sign language, gestures, and voice output devices, children can learn to request desired items, answer questions, make comments, share their feelings, and increase their participation in everyday routines.

DESIGNING TECHNOLOGICAL TEACHING PROCEDURES

The behavioral strategies discussed in this chapter can be used in conjunction with one another to develop *technological* teaching procedures to achieve specific goals for young children with ASD and other disabilities and to increase their active participation in everyday routines. When selecting strategies to use, it is important to determine whether skill performance or skill acquisition is the main goal. A child may have the skill but require motivation to use it fluently and consistently (skill performance), or the skill may not be part of the child's repertoire and explicit instruction will be required (skill acquisition). When skill performance is the goal, you can select strategies such as positive reinforcement, differential reinforceement of alternative behavior, time delay, environmental arrangements, following the child's lead, self-monitoring, and behavioral momentum. When skill acquisition is the goal, you can select strategies such as prompting/fading procedures, embedded discrete trials, modeling/request imitation, shaping, contingent imitation, balanced turn taking, task analysis, video modeling, Social Stories, and peer-mediated intervention. Of course, some strategies can be used to address both skill performance and skill acquisition.

Some teaching procedures may include only one of the strategies discussed, while others may include a variety of strategies. Table 5.2 provides a list of the strategies discussed in this chapter with a short explanation for each one for interventionists and caregivers to use as a reference when developing and implementing teaching procedures. To address *generality*, it is best to write the teaching procedures so they can be implemented across a variety of home, school, and community contexts.

Figure 5.2 shows a template for writing ABA intervention plans for domain-specific goals. Notice that there is a place to write the domain, objective, the routines that will be targeted for implementation, data collection procedures (see Chapter 6), and teaching procedures. A sample plan for one of the goals from Andrew's initial intervention program is included here. See Appendixes A through F for domain-specific sample ABA intervention plans related to social interaction, communication, positive behavior, independent play skills, daily living skills, and cognition. Keep in mind, however, that the samples provided are just that: samples. The purpose here is to provide multiple examples for writing ABA intervention plans, not to provide reproducible intervention programs. Although teams may find some of the plans relevant for specific children and may choose to use them, it will often be necessary to adapt them to meet specific needs of children and families.

INTERVENTION PLAN FOR TARGETED ROUTINES

Remember that not only can teams identify domain-specific goals and design interventions for those goals that can be implemented across a variety of everyday routines, but teams can also assess specific routines and develop routine-specific goals to enhance the child's communication skills, social interaction skills, independence, cognitive skills, and positive behaviors within the routine. Figure 5.3 provides a template for designing an intervention plan for a targeted routine. The ecological assessment discussed in Chapter 3 (see Figure 3.12) includes places to identify the routines, goals to target for communication, social interaction, and independence, cognition, and positive behaviors. There is a place to identify behavioral strategies to use for each goal. To avoid overwhelming caregivers, teaching procedures are not included. However, interventionists can certainly write out routine-specific teaching procedures if desired. Another alternative is to use the template provided and use modeling and coaching procedures discussed in Chapter 7 to assist caregivers with implementing routine-specific interventions. Figure 5.3 shows a sample routine-specific intervention plan used for Andrew's bathtime routine. See Appendixes A through F for additional examples of routine-specific intervention plans. Again, the purpose of the samples is to provide multiple examples, not to provide reproducible routine-specific interven-

Table 5.2.   Behavioral teaching strategies

Strategy	Brief explanation
Positive reinforcement	After the child engages in a desired behavior, provide a consequence that is rewarding to increase the likelihood that the behavior will occur again in the future.
Differential reinforcement of alternative behavior	Ignore the child's problem behavior and positively reinforce the child for displaying an alternative positive behavior.
Prompting/fading procedure	Provide assistance to enable the child to respond successfully, then systematically fade out the assistance provided until the child can meet the expectation independently.
Shaping	Reinforce successive approximations of a desired behavior to get the child closer and closer to the end goal.
Embedded discrete trials	Provide an antecedent (opportunity for the child to respond or initiate), prompt if necessary, and provide positive reinforcement after the child responds appropriately.
Time delay	Provide an antecedent (opportunity for the child to respond or initiate) followed by a brief wait time paired with an expectant look and expectant body language.
Task analysis/chaining	Break down a task into individual steps and teach them using forward chaining, backward chaining, or total task presentation.
Video modeling/ video self-modeling	Show the child video clips of peers or himself/herself demonstrating a desired behavior to teach the child to display the behavior shown in the video.
Self-monitoring	Teach the child how to monitor his/her performance using self-assessment tools.
Behavioral momentum	Use a pattern of easy-easy-difficult requests to increase the child's motivation to respond.
Follow the child's lead	Attend to what the child is attending to in order to establish a positive interaction.
Environmental arrangements	Place desired items out of reach, give small amounts of a desired item, do something unexpected, or adjust environmental stimuli.
Balanced turn taking	Structure interactions with the child to establish long chains of back-and-forth interactions.
Modeling/request imitation	Demonstrate what the child is expected to do, provide an opportunity for the child to imitate, and provide immediate feedback.
Contingent imitation	Imitate what the child is doing for purposes of establishing a positive interaction.
Peer-mediated intervention	Teach peers strategies for promoting positive interactions with the child.
Social Stories	Write short stories using clear statements written from the child's perspective that teach behavioral or social expectations.
Priming	Supply information to prepare a child for effective performance of a task or activity.
Augmentative and alternative communication strategies	Provide opportunities for children who are nonverbal or limited in their verbal expression to communicate using pictures, symbols, sign language, gestures, or voice output devices.

ABA Teaching Plan Template

Child's name: __Andrew_____   Domain: __Communication_____

Objective	Routines to target
When given a choice of two items, Andrew will request the desired item by pointing for 5 consecutive days.	Bath, meals and snacks, playing with toys

Data collection procedures: __Level of independence data_____

Explanation of data collection procedures:

4: Independent

3: Minimal prompting (push both items forward, use a verbal prompt, gently tap his hand)

2: Moderate prompting (push one item forward, use modeling/request imitation)

1: Maximum Prompting (gentle physical assistance)

Teaching procedures:

1. Provide an opportunity for Andrew to respond to a choice by presenting two items of interest and holding them at eye level while you're face-to-face. You can say something such as "Which one do you want?" or "Pick one." But make sure you don't say the same thing every time or he will get dependent on that as a prompt. Sometimes you may not need to say anything because holding up two items is enough of an indicator that he can choose one.
2. If Andrew points to an item, provide *positive reinforcement* by giving him the item.
3. If Andrew does not point to an item, restate the request and use *time delay* (wait with an expectant look/body language). Provide *positive reinforcement* if he responds.
4. If Andrew still does not point to an item, use the following *least-to-most prompts* hierarchy:
   a. Restate the request and push both items closer to encourage him to point to one.
   b. Restate the request and move one item forward that you think he wants and the other item back.
   c. Use *modeling/request imitation* by pointing to an item and then encourage Andrew to do the same.
   d. Use gentle physical guidance (i.e., tap Andrew's hand, gently move Andrew's hand, lightly form Andrew's hand into a point).
5. Provide *positive reinforcement* if Andrew responds, even if a prompt is required.

Figure 5.2.   Sample ABA Teaching Plan Template. A blank version of this form can be found in Appendix G.

Intervention Plan for Targeted Routine

Child's name: __Andrew__   Routine: __Bathtime__

	Goals	Behavioral strategies
Communication	1. Andrew will engage in singing songs by filling in sounds/words when his mom or sister pauses during the song.	Modeling/request imitation Time delay Positive reinforcement
Social interaction	1. Andrew will share bath toys with his sister when she asks for something with an outstretched hand. 2. Andrew will engage in a reciprocal game with his sister in the bath entailing hiding toys under the water and finding them.	Prompting/fading procedures Balanced turn taking Positive reinforcement
Independence	1. Andrew will undress himself. 2. Andrew will wash himself.	Task analysis/total task presentation Positive reinforcement
Cognition	1. Andrew will receptively identify body parts.	Embedded discrete trials Positive behaviors
Positive behaviors	N/A	

Figure 5.3. Sample Intervention Plan for Targeted Routine. A blank version of this form can be found in Appendix G.

tion plans. Routine-specific intervention plans must be individualized for the child, the family, and the specified routine.

CHAPTER SUMMARY

The strategies presented in this chapter are a sample of behavioral strategies that can be used to teach social interaction, communication, academic, behavioral, and independent functioning skills. A template for writing domain-specific ABA intervention plans was provided. In developing ABA teaching procedures, many of the strategies discussed in this chapter are used in conjunction with one another to develop systematic teaching procedures, as shown in the example provided in Figure 5.2. The most important aspects of ABA teaching procedures are that they be *conceptual* and *technological*. The procedures should include behavioral strategies such as the ones included in this chapter, and they should be written in explicit detail to ensure all caregivers implement the interventions in the same manner. This chapter also included a template for writing routine-specific intervention plans, with a sample provided. The appendixes include many more examples of domain-specific and routine-specific intervention plans.

6

Data Collection and Analysis

· ·

Data collection and analysis is a crucial component of ABA interventions in the natural environment. It is through data collection and analysis that teams can determine whether the interventions are positively affecting the child's learning. This chapter offers a rationale for data collection, descriptions of various data collection methods, sample data sheets, procedures for determining mastery, and methods for making data-based decisions when children are not making progress.

RATIONALE FOR DATA COLLECTION

Those who are familiar with ABA teaching procedures know that data collection is essential. However, the rationale for data collection is not always completely understood. In many situations where ABA interventions are being implemented, the children receive one-to-one instruction in their home, a school, or a clinic. There is often "the book" for each child receiving ABA instruction. "The book" typically includes reams of data sheets and is quite large. What some fail to understand is that data collection is not about collecting a pile of data sheets to prove that data are being collected. In fact, there is no point in taking data if the information is not graphed and analyzed regularly to make instructional decisions.

Data collection has two main purposes: to monitor progress and to determine mastery. Using data collection to monitor progress means that interventionists examine the data regularly to determine whether the child is making adequate gains. Using data collection to determine mastery means that interventionists use the data to know when the child has met the specific objective. When goals are initially written, they must include criteria for mastery, as was discussed in Chapter 4. The criteria for mastery typically indicate the data collection methods to be used. For example, if the criterion for mastery is 80% accuracy, percentage data should be collected.

When ABA teaching procedures are implemented in the natural environment with caregivers as the primary intervention providers, the methods of collecting of data must be appropriate and feasible for the caregivers to manage. There is a big difference between data collection methods that trained service providers are likely to use and methods that caregivers can use during their everyday routines. Thus, the section that follows will provide descriptions of a variety of data collection methods that are user friendly for caregivers implementing interventions in the natural environment.

DATA COLLECTION PROCEDURES FOR DOMAIN-SPECIFIC GOALS

No matter what method of data collection is selected for domain-specific goals, it is important to graph the data to allow for visual analysis. A collection of numbers and data sheets does not allow for easy interpretations of the data. When data are presented visually, you can clearly see progress or lack thereof. This allows you to make instructional decisions early on to ensure that children make adequate gains. When you meet with caregivers to review data, having visual representations of the data helps them to understand the progress their child is making. Graphing data does not need to be time-consuming. In fact, every data collection method discussed in this chapter can be adapted into a basic graph in a matter of seconds.

It is important to collect data on a regular basis. Caregivers cannot decide to take data whenever it is convenient or whenever they happen to remember. For some objectives, daily data collection is most appropriate. For others, taking data three times a week is sufficient. Even data collection once a week for certain goals may be all that is needed. However, it is necessary to continue to take data consistently and to use the same frequency of data collection week after week. Otherwise, the data may be skewed. For example, if a caregiver randomly takes data, it may turn out that data are collected only when the child performs poorly or only when the child performs extremely well. In general, it is best to take data daily if that is possible for the caregivers. Frequent data collection is much easier when caregivers have a variety of different procedures from which to select. Percentage data, level of independence data, individualized rating systems, frequency data, and yes/no data are discussed in detail next.

Percentage Data

The most commonly used method of data collection for monitoring progress and determining mastery in ABA interventions is percentage data. In the context of natural environments, however, percentage data often are not feasible for caregivers to manage. Collecting percentage data requires a trial-by-trial approach. Every time the child has an opportunity to respond, the caregiver must indicate whether the child responded correctly, incorrectly, or needed prompting. To figure out the percentage correct, the caregiver divides the number of correct responses by the total number of opportunities to respond, then multiplies the quotient by 100. While this type of data collection is the most accurate and objective method for collecting data, interventionists cannot expect caregivers to collect data in such a manner while implementing interventions within their everyday routines. It would even be difficult for highly skilled behavior analysts to collect percentage data for a variety of different goals when implementing interventions in the natural environment. Even if caregivers or interventionists could manage to collect percentage data, the constant need to use data sheets to document responses can result in less effective interventions because it interrupts the flow of reciprocal interactions with the child.

Even when it is feasible for caregivers to use percentage data collection, this method may not be appropriate for certain goals. For example, progress on many communication and social interaction goals is not easily monitored using percentage data. Consider the following goal: "Jessica will request desired items using simple sentences with 80% accuracy." Percentage data would not be the most appropriate data collection method for this goal because caregivers do not always know how many opportunities a child has in a given period of time to request desired items because they cannot get into the brains of the children to know when they actually want or need something. If the number of opportunities is unknown, collecting percentage data is not possible. Or consider this goal: "David will engage in joint play with peers during recess 70% of the time." If preschool teachers were monitoring progress for this goal using percentage data, they would need to keep track of how many minutes David engages in joint play during recess and divide that total by the total number of minutes the children are at recess. This is not a realistic data collection method for preschool teachers when they are responsible for the rest of the class during recess as well.

Although percentage data collection has limitations, this method can be used to monitor progress for one or two goals at a time without overwhelming caregivers or negatively affecting interactions between caregivers and children. Percentage data is the best option for goals such as the following:

1. The child will receptively identify primary colors in a field of two with 100% accuracy.

2. The child will expressively identify numbers 0 through 10 with 100% accuracy.

3. The child will answer simple literal questions pertaining to pictures in books with 80% accuracy.

A percentage data collection sheet is shown in Figure 6.1, with sample data from Andrew's parents. This data sheet is designed so that caregivers can either simply circle the percentage correct for the particular date or take trial-by-trial data. Taking trial-by-trial data means that each time there is an opportunity for a child to respond the caregiver will circle either "c" for correct or "i" for incorrect. "Incorrect" should also be used if the child doesn't respond at all or requires prompting to respond. The percentage correct is determined by dividing the number of correct responses by the total number of opportunities. To create a visual representation of the data, circle the percentage for each date and draw lines to connect the scores for consecutive dates.

Percentage Correct Data Sheet

Child's name: _Andrew_

Goal: _Receptively identify common objects in a field of two with 100% accuracy_

TRIALS	Date: 03/05	Date: 03/06	Date: 03/07	Date:	Date:
10	C / I 100%	C / I 100%	C / I 100%	C / I 100%	C / I 100%
9	C / I 90%	C / I 90%	C / I 90%	C / I 90%	C / I 90%
8	C / I 80%	C / I 80%	C / I (80%)	C / I 80%	C / I 80%
7	C / I 70%	C / I 70%	C / I 70%	C / I 70%	C / I 70%
6	C / I 60%	C̸ / I 60%	C / I 60%	C / I 60%	C / I 60%
5	C / I̸ 50%	C / I̸ (50%)	C̸ / I 50%	C / I 50%	C / I 50%
4	C̸ / I (40%)	C / I̸ 40%	C̸ / I 40%	C / I 40%	C / I 40%
3	C / I̸ 30%	C / I̸ 30%	C / I̸ 30%	C / I 30%	C / I 30%
2	C / I̸ 20%	C̸ / I 20%	C̸ / I 20%	C / I 20%	C / I 20%
1	C̸ / I 10%	C̸ / I 10%	C̸ / I 10%	C / I 10%	C / I 10%

Figure 6.1. Sample Percentage Correct Data Sheet. A blank version of this form can be found in Appendix G.

Although the data sheet shows ten trials, that doesn't mean there must be 10 responses each time data are collected in order to calculate a percentage. Simply divide the number of correct responses by the total number of opportunities and multiply by 100. The number of opportunities should be at least four, however, to get enough responses to ensure consistent responding. For example, a child may respond correctly the first and second time but not the third and fourth time. If the caregiver only took data on the first two trials, the child would score 100%. However, if responses were recorded for all four trials, the child's score would be 50%. Notice that the data sheet shows percentages rounded to the nearest 10% (e.g. 10%, 20%, 30%). If the score is between two percentages (e.g. 33%), simply write the actual percentage in the appropriate place (for example, write 33% between 30% and 40%) and circle the percentage. Interventionists and caregivers can also create their own percentage data sheets or use software such as Excel to input data and create graphs.

In addition to using percentage data for goals similar to the ones listed, this method of data collection can effectively be utilized for task analysis in teaching daily

Directions: Indicate whether the child performed independently or with prompting for each step. If prompting is required, indicate whether maximum, moderate, or minimal prompting was used. Divide the number of independent responses by 10 (total number of steps) and multiply by 100 to get the percentage of task completion. Record percentages on the percentage data sheet.

Steps	Independent	Maximum prompting	Moderate prompting	Minimal prompting
1. Get toothbrush.				
2. Turn on water.				
3. Wet toothbrush.				
4. Get toothpaste.				
5. Open toothpaste.				
6. Squeeze toothpaste onto toothbrush.				
7. Brush teeth.				
8. Rinse mouth with water.				
9. Rinse toothbrush and put it away.				
10. Close the toothpaste tube.				

Figure 6.2. Using percentage data collection with a task analysis for brushing teeth.

living skills. The caregiver indicates the steps of the task or routine the child performed independently and the steps for which the child required prompting. Next, the caregiver divides the number of independent steps by the total number of steps to get a percentage of task completion. This is illustrated in Figure 6.2 with an example of tooth brushing. The caregiver can use the percentage data for recording responses for the different steps without using the table if desired. That eliminates the step of transferring the percentages from the table to the percentage data sheet. A convenient feature of the table is that it allows the caregiver to indicate levels of prompting. This can show progress more quickly than task completion because while the percentages may not be going up, the levels of prompting may be decreasing.

Level of Independence Data

Level of independence data collection is simple and informative and can be used to monitor progress and document mastery for many goals and objectives. This method entails creating a rating system that indicates how much prompting the child needs to meet the expectation of the goal. Below is an example of a generic rating system that can be used for level of independence data:

1. Maximum prompting (the child requires extensive amounts of assistance and is not showing any independence)

2. Moderate prompting (the child requires assistance but shows some independence)

3. Minimal prompting (the child is almost independent but requires a small amount of assistance)

4. Independent (the child performs the skill without assistance)

When using a rating system such as this, the caregiver records the child's average performance for a given period of time. The period of time can be a whole day, a portion of a day, or a specific routine. With this data collection system, trial-by-trial data collection is not necessary. The caregiver simply records how much assistance the child required overall. For example, if the child requires maximum prompting most of the day, but there were a couple of opportunities in which the child performed with moderate levels of assistance, the caregiver should still indicate maximum prompting for that day. If you are unsure which number to record, it is better to record the lower number. This is not to suggest that you are setting low expectations for children. It is just better to err on the low side so as to avoid cutting off intervention prematurely. If a caregiver inaccurately gauges a child as independent, that data could make interventionists consider a goal mastered prematurely. When this happens, the child can lose the skill learned because fluency and maintenance of the skill were not obtained. If choosing the lower number is not desirable, another option is to record 1.5, 2.5, or 3.5 when the child is between two ratings.

Although the generic rating system described above can be used, the ratings sometimes may be too subjective. To enhance the objectivity of the data collection, it is best to define what is considered maximum, moderate, and minimal prompting by giving clear examples. Consider the following objective: "Stephen will independently respond to greetings from peers and adults using verbal and/or nonverbal responses." The prompting levels can be defined in the following manner:

1: Maximum prompting: Gentle physical assistance was needed to get Stephen to wave.

2: Moderate prompting: A verbal prompt was needed, such as "Say hello," or modeling/request imitation was needed to get Stephen to respond verbally or with a wave.

3: Minimal prompting: The greetings needed to be repeated and/or time delay needed to be used.

4: Independent: The child responded to greetings without prompts.

This type of description for each level of independence is often helpful to ensure that data are collected in a meaningful way. If caregivers are not given specific performance examples, they may not take data accurately. With specific examples, caregivers can record the ratings with much more confidence because the type of assistance provided is listed for each rating.

Figure 6.3 shows an example of a data collection sheet for level of independence data. This sheet allows caregivers to collect data for up to three different goals using a level of independence rating system. A graphical display of the data is created by simply circling the level of independence rating for each goal and drawing a line to connect to the previous day's rating. It may take as little as 10 seconds for the caregiver

Level of Independence Data Sheet

Child's name: _Andrew_

Goal	Date: 10/15	Date: 10/16	Date: 10/17	Date: 10/18	Date: 10/19	Date: 10/22	Date: 10/23	Date:
Asking for help	4	4	4	4	4	4	4	4
	3	3	3	3	3	③	③	3
	2	2	②	②	②	2	2	2
	①	①	1	1	1	1	1	1

Goal	Date:	Date:	Date:	Date:	Date:	Date:	Date:	Date:
Imitate motor movements	4	4	4	4	4	4	4	4
	3	3	3	3	3	③	3	3
	2	②	②	②	②	2	②	2
	①	1	1	1	1	1	1	1

Goal	Date:	Date:	Date:	Date:	Date:	Date:	Date:	Date:
	4	4	4	4	4	4	4	4
	3	3	3	3	3	3	3	3
	2	2	2	2	2	2	2	2
	1	1	1	1	1	1	1	1

1 = Maximum prompting   2 = Moderate prompting   3 = Minimal prompting
4 = Independent

Figure 6.3. Sample Level of Independence Data Sheet. A blank version of this form can be found in Appendix G.

to record a child's level of independence data each day, depending on how many goals the child has.

Individualized Rating System

Interventionists can also develop an individualized rating system if the level of independence rating system is not appropriate or meaningful. The same data collection sheet can be used as for level of independence, but the numbers can represent something else. Consider this objective: "Marla will imitate all consonant and vowel sounds to provide the initial sound for items she wants or sees." Notice that the word "all" is used to indicate the criterion for mastery. An individualized rating system such as the one below can be used to measure progress toward this goal:

0:    Marla does not imitate any consonant or vowel sounds.

1:    Marla imitates very few consonant and vowel sounds.

2:    Marla imitates many consonant and vowel sounds.

3:    Marla imitates most consonant and vowel sounds.

4:    Marla imitates all consonant and vowel sounds.

Of course the data collection sheet should include numbers 0–4 instead of 1–4 if you are using a rating system such as the one above. Although it is generally easier to stick with a generic level of independence rating system, there will be some objectives that require a more original way to measure progress. For example, the objective "Alex will respond to play initiations from peers and adults across a variety of home and school contexts" would probably be best monitored using an individualized rating system that includes number ranges such as the following:

0:    Does not respond to any play initiations

1:    Responds to play initiations from adults only

2:    Responds to play initiations from adults and peers for a few specific activities

3:    Responds to play initiations from adults and peers for most activities

4:    Responds to play initiations from adults and peers for all activities

Frequency Data Collection

For some objectives, frequency data collection is most appropriate. This entails recording the number of times something occurs. Consider the following objective: "Brian will initiate play with a peer at least twice each day at school." It would be easier for the teacher to record the number of times Brian initiates play with a peer than to try to figure out some sort of percentage. If the criterion for mastery indicates a number, that usually means that frequency data is the best way to monitor progress toward meeting the

Frequency Data Sheet

Child's name: _Andrew_

Goal: _Sound imitation_

	Date 5/01	Date 5/02	Date 5/03	Date 5/04	Date	Date
Total number	10	10	10	10	10	10
of sounds imitated	9	9	9	9	9	9
	8	8	8	8	8	8
per day	7	7	7	7	7	7
	6	6	6	6	6	6
	5	5	5	5	5	5
	4	4	(4)	4	4	4
	(3)	3	3	(3)	3	3
	1	(2)	1	1	2	2
	1	1	1	1	1	1
	0	0	0	0	0	0

Figure 6.4. Sample Frequency Data Sheet. A blank version of this form can be found in Appendix G.

goal. Figure 6.4 provides a sample frequency data collection sheet. The caregiver can use it by putting a slash through a number each time the child displays the specific behavior. For example, when Brian initiates play with a peer the first time, the caregiver or preschool teacher puts a slash through the number 1. Each time Brian initiates play after that, the caregiver can put a slash through the next number. After the time period is over (whole day, school day, routine), the caregiver circles the total number of times Brian initiated play with a peer. The circled number for each column is connected with a line to the ones before and after it to create a graphical display of the data for purposes of monitoring progress and determining mastery.

Another way to use frequency data is to transfer running lists into frequency counts. Consider this goal: "Jasmine will request at least five different preferred items by naming the item." Caregivers can keep a running list of the items Jasmine requests by naming them. The interventionist can transfer the number of items on the list to a frequency data sheet by recording the total number of items on the list. When using this method, however, it is recommended that the caregiver write the word on the list the first time the child uses it independently, and then put a tally mark next to the word each time the child uses the word again in the future. The word should not be included in the frequency count until the child uses it at least five times. This ensures that the data show consistent responses and not just responses that occurred once or twice.

Yes/No Data Collection

Some objectives will simply require the caregiver to record whether or not the specific behavior was demonstrated. Consider the following goal: "Without prompting, Jamie will greet at least one peer upon entering the classroom each morning." For this objective, the preschool teacher would only need to indicate "yes" if Jamie greeted a peer or "no" if Jamie did not greet a peer or needed prompting to do so. Here are some other goals for which yes/no data may be used to monitor progress:

1. The child will take one bite of a new food item when it is presented on her plate at dinnertime for 7 consecutive days.

2. The child will stay buckled in the car seat when the car is in motion for 2 consecutive weeks.

3. The child will sleep through the night without coming out of the bedroom for 5 consecutive nights.

Figure 6.5 shows an example of a data collection sheet that can be used in recording yes/no data. The caregiver simply circles "y" or "n" and draws a line to connect the circle for the previous date to the current date to create a graphical representation of the data.

SELECTING A DATA COLLECTION PROCEDURE

There is no set rule regarding which type of data collection procedure to use for each goal written for a child. However, interventionists can consider several things when deciding how to encourage caregivers to collect data. The first thing to consider is how the criterion for mastery is stated. If the criterion for mastery indicates a percentage, then percentage data collection should be used. If the criterion indicates that the child will demonstrate the skill independently (or without prompting), then level of independence data should be used. If the criterion includes a specific behavioral expectation, then an individualized rating system or yes/no data may be appropriate. If the criterion indicates that the behavior should be displayed a specific number of times during a given time period, then frequency data can be taken.

Another consideration when selecting a data collection procedure is ease of use. Since a caregiver is the one responsible for data collection, the methods of collecting data must be compatible with the responsibilities the caregiver has throughout the day. Level of independence data is probably the easiest and quickest way for caregivers to collect meaningful data. It does take time initially to determine what each level of independence rating means for each goal, but after that, it is just a matter of circling a

Yes/No Data Collection Sheet

Child's name: _Andrew_

Goal	Date 1/10	Date 1/11	Date 1/12	Date 1/13	Date 1/14	Date 1/15	Date 1/16	Date	Date
Eat a cup of yogurt with a spoon independently	Y / Ⓝ	Y / Ⓝ	Y / Ⓝ	Ⓨ / N	Y / Ⓝ	Ⓨ / N	Ⓨ / N	Y / N	Y / N
Walk next to Mom during neighborhood walks (without running ahead)	Y / Ⓝ	Y / Ⓝ	Ⓨ / N	Ⓨ / N	Ⓨ / N	Ⓨ / N	Ⓨ / N	Y / N	Y / N
	Y / N	Y / N	Y / N	Y / N	Y / N	Y / N	Y / N	Y / N	Y / N
	Y / N	Y / N	Y / N	Y / N	Y / N	Y / N	Y / N	Y / N	Y / N

Figure 6.5.   Sample Yes/No Data Collection Sheet. A blank version of this form can be found in Appendix G.

number at the end of the day for each goal that uses level of independence to monitor progress. Individualized rating scales and yes/no data are also very easy for caregivers to use. Frequency data may be a little more challenging, and as was mentioned earlier, collecting percentage data typically is the most difficult method to use on an ongoing basis. When percentage data are preferred, however, data can be collected once a week or biweekly instead of daily to ease the burden on caregivers.

One last thing to consider when selecting a data collection procedure is how you plan to teach the skill. For example, if prompting/fading procedures will be used to teach the skill, then using level of independence data collection makes perfect sense since the caregiver records how much prompting was needed. If task analysis is used to teach a skill, caregivers can record percentage data by taking the number of steps the child completed independently and dividing that by the total number of steps to get a percentage. In the end, there may be many options for meaningful data collection for any particular goal. The team should select a method that allows progress to be shown and is easy for the caregivers to use.

DETERMINING MASTERY

Chapter 4 discussed writing objectives so that they include a criterion for mastery. Collecting data allows interventionists to determine when mastery has been achieved. There is no rule regarding how long a child should display a certain skill for it to be considered mastered. The criterion for mastery may depend on how often data are collected. If data are collected daily, it may be best to have at least five consecutive days of data at the mastery level before indicating the objective is mastered. When goals are implemented in preschools, many times children will achieve mastery Wednesday, Thursday, and Friday because they had Monday and Tuesday to learn a specific skill, but when they come back to school after the weekend, they are no longer at the mastery level. Thus, waiting for five consecutive days of mastery ensures that the child maintained the skill over the weekend. On the other hand, if data were not being collected daily, having five consecutive days to determine mastery would not be appropriate. If data are collected three times a week, mastery can be determined when the student is performing the skill independently for three consecutive data points. If data are being collected weekly, it may be most appropriate to indicate mastery when the student performs the desired skill for four consecutive weeks. It is up to the team to decide what criterion for mastery is most appropriate, but it is important to be sure that mastery is not indicated too early because the child may not have fully learned what was expected and may still require explicit instruction and progress monitoring.

RESPONDING TO LACK OF PROGRESS

Remember that one of the dimensions of ABA is that the interventions must be *effective* (see Chapter 2). That means that if the child is not progressing, changes must be made. Also remember that the main purpose of data collection is to monitor progress so that interventionists can make instructional decisions. If progress is not being made, something must be done to address the problem. Many interventionists immediately assume that the teaching procedures should be changed if the child is not making progress, but before making that assumption, it's a good idea to ask the following questions:

- Have the procedures been implemented correctly?

- Have the data been collected properly?

- Does the data collection procedure need to be changed?

- Do the teaching procedures need to be changed or altered?

- Does the goal need to be changed or altered?

Procedures for implementing ABA interventions should be technological, which means that there are written procedures to follow when teaching the specific skill. If progress is not being made, it is important to first find out whether the procedures are actually being implemented as planned. If the answer is no, the caregiver may need some more support from the interventionist to learn how to implement the teaching procedures.

If it is determined that the teaching procedures are being implemented correctly, the next step is to determine whether data are being collected properly. Sometimes it may seem that progress is not being made, but in fact the caregiver is simply not collecting data in a consistent or correct manner. If data are being collected correctly but the caregiver says something such as, "I know my child is making progress, but the data are not showing the improvements," the data collection method may need to be changed. For example, if percentages are being used and the child is scoring 0% consistently and seemingly not making progress, it may be helpful to switch to level of independence data collection to be able to show whether or not the child is learning to be more independent and to require less assistance from the caregiver.

If data collection is not the problem, then the next step is to determine whether the teaching procedures should be changed or altered. There is no one set way to teach any skill, so if something isn't working you can design a different set of teaching procedures. But keep in mind that the teaching procedures must still be *conceptual* and utilize principles of behavior. If progress is still not being made after the teaching procedures have been changed multiple times, it may be appropriate to consider changing or altering the goal. Perhaps the goal is not developmentally appropriate for the child and there is a prerequisite skill that must be taught first.

DATA COLLECTION PROCEDURES FOR ROUTINE-SPECIFIC INTERVENTIONS

Data collection for routine-specific goals is different from what is used for domain-specific goals. To assess the child's progress during specific routines, the early intervention provider will conduct the ecological assessment for the targeted routine repeatedly throughout the intervention process to assess the child's growth (see Chapter 3, Figure 3.12). This can be done monthly, bimonthly, or even weekly, depending on the preferences of the team. Each time an ecological assessment is conducted, the early intervention provider will determine whether new goals should be set and/or different behavioral strategies should be used.

CHAPTER SUMMARY

Data collection and analysis allow interventionists to monitor progress and determine when mastery has been achieved. By using data collection methods discussed in this chapter, caregivers can easily document their child's performance to allow interventionists to make data-based instructional decisions.

7

Putting It All Together

. . . .

Now it's time to take everything discussed in this book and show how it all fits together. Suggestions are provided for the roles individual team members will play in assessment, setting goals, designing interventions, implementing interventions during everyday routines, and evaluating the child's progress. This book provides so many different options for assessment and intervention planning that it may be overwhelming for some teams. Thus, this chapter describes different ways teams can utilize the information in this book to suit their needs. The chapter concludes with a discussion about whether one-to-one ABA therapy should be considered for some children in addition to ABA interventions in the natural environment.

ROLES OF TEAM MEMBERS

Although early intervention teams may align roles differently, this chapter provides some general guidelines for aligning roles when developing ABA interventions that will be implemented during everyday routines. The term *early intervention provider* will be used to represent any professional who may serve as the primary service provider during the process. This person may be a special education teacher, a speech-language pathologist, an occupational or physical therapist, a service coordinator, or a board-certified behavior analyst (BCBA). Ideally, the primary service provider would be a BCBA or at least a professional with extensive training and experience in designing and implementing ABA interventions. If the primary service provider does not have a strong background in ABA, it is recommended that a BCBA provide some supervision and support throughout the process. Other team members discussed in this chapter include caregivers (family members and preschool teachers when applicable) and related service providers.

Roles During the Assessment Process

During the assessment process the early intervention provider serves as the facilitator involving other team members in gathering information related to the child's strengths and interests, present levels of performance in communication, social interaction, independent play skills, daily living skills, and/or cognitive skills, behavioral challenges, and participation across a variety of everyday routines (see Chapter 3). The caregivers should be heavily involved in this process to provide the early intervention provider with as much specific information about the child as possible. The early intervention provider can conduct caregiver interviews and direct observations of the child with the caregivers in the natural environment.

If the child attends a preschool, the preschool teacher should also have the opportunity to share information with the early intervention provider, and the early intervention provider should conduct observations at the preschool. Related service providers such as speech/language pathologists, occupational therapists, and physical therapists should also be included in the assessment process to provide information to the early intervention provider about the child's present levels of performance related to their areas of specialization. These professionals can join the early intervention provider during interviews and direct observations and can also provide written reports from independent evaluations.

It is the responsibility of the early intervention provider to summarize all of the information gathered through interviews, direct observations, and written reports, and share the results with the entire team. Once the assessment information is shared, the early intervention provider should ask the caregivers to identify their priorities for the child.

Roles During Goal Setting

The early intervention provider should facilitate the goal setting process. Using the assessment information gathered and the priorities identified by the caregivers, the early intervention provider should suggest domain-specific goals to the team. The goals should be written using the criteria discussed in Chapter 4, and all team members should have opportunities to review the suggested goals and offer changes or additions. Once the goals have been agreed upon, the caregivers should select the goal(s) they would like to address first.

When setting goals for specific routines, the early intervention provider should do so in collaboration with the caregiver. This is best done immediately following the assessment of a specific routine. The early intervention provider should summarize the child's present participation in the routine, ask the caregivers to share some possible goals for increasing the child's engagement, social interaction, and independence within the routine, and then offer any additional suggestions for goals that can be targeted during the routine. The caregivers should then select the goals they would like to target for the routine selected.

Roles When Designing ABA Interventions

The early intervention provider will be primarily responsible for designing the domain-specific and routine-specific ABA intervention plans. As was mentioned earlier, if the early intervention provider is not a BCBA, it is recommended that intervention plans be designed in collaboration with someone who is a BCBA. Although the early intervention provider will be the one responsible for designing the interventions, caregivers and preschool teachers, when applicable, should be involved in selecting strategies whenever possible. There are often many different possibilities for designing interventions, and the individuals who will be implementing the interventions should be comfortable with the procedures selected.

Roles During Implementation

Caregivers will be the individuals primarily responsible for implementing the ABA interventions in the natural environment. However, the early intervention provider delivers training, models how to implement the interventions, and coaches caregivers as they learn how to deliver the interventions within their everyday routines.

Training   It is recommended that the early intervention provider deliver training before caregivers begin implementation of an ABA intervention. The training can and should be goal-specific. Although it may be helpful to provide an overview of ABA teaching strategies, it is essential that the caregivers and teachers receive specific training from the early intervention provider on how to use the strategies to target specific goals. During the training the early intervention provider should provide a written intervention plan (see Chapter 5), describe the intervention in explicit detail, model how to implement the intervention, and provide opportunities for the caregivers to demonstrate how to implement the intervention and receive immediate feedback from the intervention provider.

Modeling   After the caregivers receive training for a specific ABA intervention, the early intervention provider should model how to implement the intervention in the natural environment with the child during the actual routine(s) targeted. It is helpful to have the caregivers videotape the early intervention provider modeling the intervention so that they will be able to review the procedures as often as they need to do so. After modeling the intervention in the natural environment, the early intervention provider should summarize what was shown, giving specific examples from the actual routine and providing an opportunity for the caregivers to ask questions related to the procedures.

Coaching   After the early intervention provider models an ABA intervention, the caregivers should immediately have an opportunity to implement the intervention and receive feedback and support from the early intervention provider. Many early intervention providers may think they can just show caregivers what to do and then they will be able to do it. It is not that simple. Early intervention providers have education, training, and experience with implementing ABA interventions, but caregivers almost always do not. What may seem easy to an early intervention provider may be quite difficult for caregivers. Therefore, caregivers should be coached through the process of learning how to implement an intervention by allowing them time to practice implementing the intervention while the early intervention provider is on hand to let them know what they did correctly and what they should adjust the next time. Caregivers should not be expected to implement any intervention until they have demonstrated proficiency during coaching sessions with the early intervention provider.

Coaching doesn't end when the caregivers are ready to implement the interventions during their everyday routines. Early intervention providers should provide continual coaching throughout the implementation process. This can be done through scheduled direct observations with opportunities for the caregiver to receive feedback from the early intervention provider. Coaching can also be done using a video-stimulated recall protocol (Leach & LaRocque, 2011). When using video-stimulated recall, the caregivers capture video of themselves implementing the interventions during their everyday routines. When the early intervention provider meets with the caregivers, they review the video together. The early intervention provider should have the caregivers point out the procedures they are using effectively and also point out anything that doesn't seem to be working. As the caregivers reflect on their implementation of the intervention, the early intervention provider should provide additional feedback related to what the caregivers did well and what they can improve next time. Video-stimulated recall provides opportunities for early intervention providers to support caregivers even when they cannot physically be present during the occurrence of the routines. It is also a great way for caregivers to learn by reflecting on their own practices with support from the early intervention provider.

Roles When Evaluating Progress

When interventions are designed, the early intervention provider selects data collection procedures for all domain-specific goals to be used to monitor the child's progress (see Chapter 6). The procedures selected should be as easy as possible for the caregivers to use within the context of their everyday routines. Early intervention providers should clearly explain to the caregivers how to collect data for each goal and should supply caregivers with the data sheets needed. It is best to give caregivers a binder that contains the assessment information, a list of domain-specific goals, ABA intervention plans for domain-specific goals, and data sheets to use for domain-specific goals. When caregivers are learning a new intervention, the early intervention provider may not suggest that the caregivers collect data immediately but instead wait until the caregivers are no longer overwhelmed with learning the new intervention. Early intervention providers can suggest daily, biweekly, or weekly data collection. It depends on the goals targeted and on the caregivers' willingness and ability to collect data consistently. Early intervention providers can collect data during their visits as well to supplement the data collected by the caregivers. The early intervention provider should review data consistently to make instructional decisions and to determine when mastery has been achieved.

VARIOUS OPTIONS FOR
UTILIZING INFORMATION IN THIS BOOK

Ideally, teams would use all of the assessment and intervention procedures shared throughout this book to develop intensive ABA intervention programs in the natural environment to meet the needs of young children with ASD and other disabilities. However, doing so may be overwhelming for some teams due to time constraints, training, and experience. With that in mind, teams may decide to assess and plan only for domain-specific goals or they may decide to assess and plan only for routine-specific goals. In any case, it is important to keep in mind the recommendation from the National Research Council (2001) that children with ASD receive at least 25 hours of intervention per week. This can be an end goal for teams to reach, but it may take time to build up the caregivers' capacity to implement intensive interventions throughout the child's week.

Domain-Specific Assessment and Goals Only

Teams may choose only to assess specific domains and set domain-specific goals rather than also assessing everyday routines and setting routine-specific goals. The interventions designed would still be implemented during everyday routines, of course. Additionally, teams may decide to assess one or two specific domains instead of assessing all domains. In some cases, teams may decide to target only one goal at a time if they feel that is all the caregivers can handle during the initial stages of learning how to embed ABA interventions within their everyday routines.

Ecological Assessments of Routines Only

Teams may choose to assess only specific routines and to set routine-specific goals rather than also assessing specific domains and setting domain-specific goals. This may be appropriate for children with less significant impairments and delays who may not require as much intensity of intervention. This option is not recommended for children with ASD because they will need specific skills targeted in the social interaction and communication domains with a great deal of intensity of interventions planned throughout their day. Teams may decide to assess and plan interventions for only one routine initially if they feel that is all the caregivers can handle until they get more comfortable with implementing ABA interventions during their everyday routines.

WHAT ABOUT ONE-TO-ONE ABA THERAPY?

This book focused on developing ABA interventions for implementation within everyday routines. Teams may question whether natural environment ABA interventions are sufficient for children with ASD and other disabilities. Although there is no absolute answer to that question, there are some things to consider if the question comes up. First, it is best to begin with natural environment ABA interventions and if—and only if—the child is not making significant gains, consider whether additional one-to-one ABA therapy may be needed. If a child is making adequate gains within the context of the natural environment, there is no reason to remove the child from natural environments to receive one-to-one ABA therapy to learn skills they may or may not generalize to the natural environment. Chapter 1 included a discussion about the different profiles of children with ASD. Some children who have severe communication impairments, social interaction impairments, cognitive impairments, attention-related difficulties, and/or anxiety issues may require some one-to-one ABA therapy to build the skills they need to benefit the most from NEI. If the team deems it necessary it have some one-to-one ABA therapy, Travis Thompson's book, *Individualized Autism Intervention for Young Children: Blending Discrete Trial and Naturalistic Strategies* (2011), can be used in conjunction with this book to help teams create a blended early intervention program with some one-to-one therapy used in addition to routines-based interventions.

Secondly, if it is deemed that some one-to-one ABA therapy is needed due to lack of progress or the child's individual profile, it is best to view natural environment ABA intervention as the primary intervention and the one-to-one therapy as the supplemental intervention. Many professionals and caregivers may view one-to-one ABA therapy as the primary intervention and anything caregivers implement as supplemental, but this does a huge disservice to families. The primary focus of early intervention is to help caregivers feel competent and confident in meeting the needs of their children. If caregivers do not feel empowered to meet the needs of their children and instead view outside ABA providers as the sole source of intervention, the lasting effects of the ABA interventions will not be as significant as when the caregivers are learning how to change the ways they interact with their child to enhance the child's development. The caregivers are the only constants in the child's life. It is the early interventionist's responsibility to teach them how to support the child's learning throughout the lifespan. Finally, if the caregivers are unwilling or unable to implement the ABA interventions within the natural environment, one-to-one ABA therapy may be necessary. While this is not ideal, one-to-one ABA therapy is better than no ABA interventions at all.

CHAPTER SUMMARY

This chapter has discussed the different roles that team members should play in assessment, setting goals, designing interventions, and evaluating the child's progress. It has also described different options for utilizing the information in this book for teams that may be overwhelmed with all of the available assessment and intervention methods and procedures. Finally, the chapter has concluded with a discussion of circumstances when teams should consider one-to-one ABA therapy in addition to ABA interventions in the natural environment. In conclusion, it is essential for teams to keep in mind that all young children learn best during naturally occurring daily routines, children with ASD and other disabilities often require intensive interventions in order to fully engage in daily routines and make significant developmental gains, and ABA interventions have a solid research base and can be used when implementing interventions in the natural environment for young children with ASD and other disabilities.

References

American Psychiatric Association. (2000). *Diagnostic and statistical manual of mental disorders* (4th ed., text rev.). Washington, DC.

Atkins-Burnett, S., & Allen-Meares, P. (2000). Infants and toddlers with disabilities: Relationship-based approaches. *Social Work, 45*(4), 371–380.

Baer, D.M., Wolf, M.M., & Risley, T.F. (1968). Some current dimensions of applied behavior analysis. *Journal of Applied Behavior Analysis, 1*, 91–97.

Baer, D.M., Wolf, M.M., & Risley, T.F. (1987). Some still-current dimensions of applied behavior analysis. *Journal of Applied Behavior Analysis, 20*, 313–327.

Bailey, J.S., & Burch, M.R. (2002). *Research methods in applied behavior analysis*. Thousand Oaks, CA: Sage Publications.

Bailey, J.S., & Burch, M.R. (2011). *Ethics for behavior analysts: Second expanded edition*. New York, NY: Routledge.

Bainbridge, N., & Smith Myles, B. (1999). The use of priming to introduce toilet training to a child with autism. *Focus on Autism and Other Developmental Disabilities, 14*(2), 106–109.

Baldwin, D.A. (1995). Understanding the link between joint attention and language. In C. Moore & P.J. Dunham (Eds.), *Joint attention: Its origins and role in development* (pp. 131–158). Hillsdale, NJ: Erlbaum.

Bayley, N. (2005). *Bayley Scales of Infant and Toddler Development, Third Edition* (Bayley-III). San Antonio, TX: Pearson.

Bellini, S. (2006). *Building social relationships: A systematic approach to teaching social interaction skills to children and adolescents with autism spectrum disorders and other social difficulties.* Shawnee Mission, KS: Autism Asperger Publishing.

Bellini, S., Akullian, J., & Hopf, A. (2007). Increasing social engagement in young children with autism spectrum disorders using video self-modeling. *School Psychology Review, 36*(1), 80–90.

Bondy, A., & Frost, L. (1994). The Picture Exchange Communication System. *Focus on Autistic Behavior, 9*(3), 1–19.

Bondy, A., & Frost, L. (2001). The Picture Exchange Communication System. *Behavior Modification, 25*(5), 725–744.

Boulware, G., Schwartz, I., Sandall, S., & McBride, B. (2006). Project DATA for toddlers: An inclusive approach to very young children with autism spectrum disorder. *Topics in Early Childhood Special Education, 26*(2), 94–105.

Bricker, D. (2001). The natural environment: A useful construct? *Infants and Young Children, 13*(4), 21–31.

Brigance, A.I. (2004). *Brigance Inventory of Early Development II* (IED II). Curriculum Associates.

Browder, D.M. (1987). *Assessment of individuals with severe handicaps*. Baltimore, MD: Paul H. Brookes Publishing Co.

Buffington, D.M., Krantz, P.J., McClannahan, L.E., & Poulson, C.L. (1998). Procedures for teaching appropriate gestural communication skills to children with autism. *Journal of Autism and Developmental Disorders, 28*(6), 535–545.

Cautilli, J., & Dziewolska, H. (2005). Brief report: Can contingent imitation reinforce trunk lifting in a three-month-old infant? *The Behavior Analyst Today, 6*(4), 229–230.

Chai, A.Y., Zhang, C., & Bisberg, M. (2006). Rethinking natural environment practice: Implications from examining various interpretations and approaches. *Early Childhood Education Journal, 34*(3), 203–208.

Chan, J.M., & O'Reilly, M.F. (2008). A Social Stories™ intervention package for students with autism in inclusive classroom settings. *Journal of Applied Behavior Analysis, 41*(3), 405–409.

Constantino, J.N., Davis, S.A., Todd, R.D., Schindler, M.K., Gross, M.M., Brophy, S.L., . . . Reich, W. (2003). Validation of a brief quantitative measure of autistic traits: Comparison of the Social Responsiveness Scale with the Autism Diagnostic Interview-Revised. *Journal of Autism & Developmental Disorders, 33*(4), 427–433.

Constantino, J.N., & Gruber, C.P. (2005). *Social Responsiveness Scale* (SRS). Torrance, CA: Western Psychological Services.

Cooper, J.O., Heron, T.E., & Heward, W.L. (2007). *Applied behavior analysis.* Englewood Cliffs, NJ: Prentice Hall.

Coyle, C., & Cole, P. (2004). A videotaped self-modeling and self-monitoring treatment program to treat off-task behavior in children with autism. *Journal of Intellectual and Developmental Disability, 29*(1), 3–15.

Davis, C.A., Brady, M.P., Hamilton, R., McEvoy, M.A., & Williams, R.E. (1994). Effects of high-probability requests on the social interactions of young children with severe disabilities. *Journal of Applied Behavior Analysis, 27,* 619–637.

Dipipi, C.M., Jitendra, A.K., & Miller, J.A. (2001). Reducing repetitive speech: Effects of strategy instruction. *Preventing School Failure, 45*(4), 177–181.

DiSalvo, C.A., & Oswald, D.P. (2002). Peer-mediated interventions to increase the social interaction of children with autism: Consideration of peer expectancies. *Focus on Autism and Other Developmental Disabilities, 17*(4), 198–207.

Dowrick, P. (1999). A review of self-modeling and related interventions. *Applied and Preventive Psych, 8,* 23–39.

Dunst, C.J., Hamby, D., Trivette, C.M., Raab, M., & Bruder, M.B. (2000). Everyday family and community life and children's naturally occurring learning opportunities. *Journal of Early Intervention, 23,* 151–164.

Dunst, C.J., & Trivette, C.M. (2001). *Parenting supports and resources, helpgiving practices, and parenting competence.* Asheville, NC: Winterberry Press.

Dunst, C.J., Trivette, C.M., & Masiello, T. (2011). Exploratory investigation of the effects of interest-based learning on the development of young children with autism. *Autism: The International Journal of Research & Practice, 15*(3), 295–305.

Ganz, J. (2008). Self-monitoring across age and ability levels: Teaching students to implement their own positive behavioral interventions. *Preventing School Failure, 53*(1), 39–48.

Ganz, J.B., & Simpson, R.L. (2004). Effects on communicative requesting and speech development of the picture exchange communication system in children with characteristics of autism. *Journal of Autism and Developmental Disorders, 34*(4), 395–409.

Gazdag, G., & Warren, S.F. (2000). Effects of adult contingent imitation on development of young children's vocal imitation. *Journal of Early Intervention, 23,* 24–35.

Gray, C.A., & Garand, J.D. (1993). Social Stories: Improving responses of students with autism with accurate social information. *Focus on Autistic Behavior, 8,* 1–10.

Greenspan, S.I., & Weider, S. (1998). *The child with special needs: Encouraging intellectual and emotional growth.* Reading, MA: Addison-Wesley.

Gresham, F.M., & MacMillan, D.L. (1998). Early intervention projects: Can its claims be substantiated and its effects replicated? *Journal of Autism and Developmental Disorders, 28,* 5–13.

Gutstein, S.E., Burgess, A.F., & Montfort, K. (2007). Evaluation of the Relationship Development Intervention program. *Autism: The International Journal of Research and Practice, 11*(5), 397–411.

Jones, E.A., & Carr, E.G. (2004). Joint attention in children with autism: Theory and intervention. *Focus on Autism & Other Developmental Disabilities, 19,* 13–26.

Halle, J.W., Marshall, A.M., & Spradlin, J.E. (1979). Time delay: A technique to increase language use and facilitate generalization in retarded children. *Journal of Applied Behavior Analysis, 14,* 389–409.

Haney, M., & Cavallaro, C.C. (1996). Using ecological assessment in daily program planning for children with disabilities in typical preschool settings. *Topics in Early Childhood Special Education, 16,* 66–81.

Hart, B.M., & Risley, T.R. (1975). Incidental teaching of language in preschool. *Journal of Applied Behavior Analysis, 8,* 411–420.

Hresko, W.P., Peak, P.K., Herron, S.R., & Bridges, D.L. (2000). *Young Children's Achievement Test* (YCAT). Torrance, CA: Western Psychological Services.

Individuals with Disabilities Education Improvement Act (IDEIA) of 2004, PL 108-446, 20 U.S.C. §§ 1400 et seq.

Jung, S., Sainato, D.M., & Davis, C.A. (2008). Using high-probability request sequences to increase social interactions in young children with autism. *Journal of Early Intervention, 30*(3), 163–187.

Kashinath, S., Woods, J., & Goldstein, H. (2006). Enhancing generalized teaching strategy use in daily routines by parents of children with autism. *Journal of Speech, Language & Hearing Research, 49*(3), 466–485.

Kates-McElrath, K., & Axelrod, S. (2006). Behavioral intervention for autism: A distinction between two behavior analytic approaches. *The Behavior Analyst Today, 7*(2), 242–252.

Koegel, L.K., & Koegel, R.L. (1995). Motivating communication in children with autism. In E. Schopler & G.B. Mesibov (Eds.), *Learning and cognition in autism* (pp. 73–87). New York, NY: Kluwer Academic/Plenum Publishers.

Koegel, L.K., Koegel, R.L., Harrower, J.K., & Carter, C.M. (1999). Pivotal Response Intervention I: Overview of approach. *Journal of Applied Behavior Analysis, 25*, 341–354.

Koegel, L.K., Koegel, R.L., Hurley, C., & Frea, W.D. (1992). Improving social skills and disruptive behavior in children with autism through self-management. *Journal of Applied Behavior Analysis, 25*, 341–353.

Koegel, R.L., & Koegel, L.K. (2006). *Pivotal Response Treatments for autism: Communication, social and academic achievement.* Baltimore: Paul H. Brookes Publishing Co.

Layer, S.A., Hanley, G.P., Heal, N.A., & Tiger, J.H. (2008). Determining individual preschoolers' preferences in a group arrangement. *Journal of Applied Behavior Analysis, 41,* 25–37.

Leach, D., & LaRocque, M. (2011). Increasing social reciprocity of young children with autism. *Intervention in School and Clinic, 46,* 150–156.

Lovaas, O.I. (1987). Behavioral treatment and normal educational and intellectual functioning in young autistic children. *Journal of Counseling and Clinical Psychology, 55,* 3–9.

Lovaas, O.I. (2003). *Teaching individuals with developmental delays: Basic intervention techniques.* Austin, TX: Pro-Ed, Inc.

Lovaas, O.I., Ackerman, A., Alexander, D., Firestone, P., Perkins, J., & Young, D. (1981). *Teaching developmentally disabled children: The ME book.* Austin, TX: Pro-Ed, Inc.

MacDonald, J.D., & Carroll, J.Y. (1992). A social partnership model for assessing early communication development: An intervention model for preconversational children. *Language, Speech, and Hearing Services in Schools, 23,* 113–124.

MacDonald, R., Anderson, J., Dube, W.V., Geckeler, A., Green, G., Holcomb, W., et al. (2006). Behavioral assessment of joint attention: A methodological report. *Research in Developmental Disabilities, 27,* 138–150.

Mace, F.C., & Belfiore, P. (1990). Behavioral momentum in the treatment of escape-motivated stereotypy. *Journal of Applied Behavior Analysis, 23,* 507–514.

Maurice, C., Green, G., & Luce, S. (Eds.) (1996). *Behavioral intervention for young children with autism: A manual for parents and professionals.* Austin, TX: Pro-Ed, Inc.

McBride, B.J., & Schwartz, I.S. (2003). Effects of teaching early interventionists to use discrete trials during ongoing classroom activities. *Topics in Early Childhood Special Education, 23*(1), 5–17.

McGee, G.G., Almeida, M.C., Sulzer-Azaroff, B., & Feldman, R.S. (1992). Promoting reciprocal interactions via peer incidental teaching. *Journal of Applied Behavior Analysis, 25*(1), 117–126.

McGee, G.G., Krantz. P.J., & McClannahan. L.E. (1985). The facilitative effects of incidental teaching on preposition use by autistic children. *Journal of Applied Behavior Analysis, 18,* 17–31.

McGee, G.G., Morrier, M.J., & Daly, T. (1999). An incidental teaching approach to early intervention for toddlers with autism. *Journal of the Association for Persons with Severe Handicaps, 24,* 133–146.

McWilliam, R.A. (2010). *Routines-based early intervention: Supporting young children and their families.* Baltimore, MD: Paul H. Brookes Publishing Co.

McWilliam, R.A., Casey, A.M., & Sims, J. (2009). The routines-based interview: A method for gathering information and assessing needs. *Infants and Young Children, 22,* 224–233.

Mirenda, P. (2003). Toward functional augmentative and alternative communication for students with autism: Manual signs, graphic symbols, and voice output communication aids. *Language, Speech, and Hearing Services in Schools, 34,* 203–216.

Morrison, L., Kamps, D., Garcia, J., & Parker, D. (2001). Peer mediation and monitoring strategies to improve initiations and social skills for students with autism. *Journal of Positive Behavior Interventions, 3*(4), 237–250.

Mundy, P. (1995). Joint attention and social-emotional approach behavior in children with autism. *Development and Psychopathology, 7,* 63–82.

Mundy, P., Sigman, M., & Kasari, C. (1990). A longitudinal study of joint attention and language development in autistic children. *Journal of Autism and Developmental Disorders, 20,* 115–128.

National Association for the Education of Young Children (NAEYC). (2012). The core of DAP. Retrieved from www.naeyc.org/dap/core

National Research Council, Committee on Educational Interventions for Children with Autism. (2001). *Educating children with autism.* Washington, DC: National Academy Press.

Partington, J.W. (2007) *The Assessment of Basic Language and Learning Skills-Revised* (ABLLS-R). Walnut Creek, CA: The Behavior Analysts.

Pierce, K., & Schreibman, L. (1994). Teaching daily living skills to children with autism in unsupervised settings through pictorial self-management. *Journal of Applied Behavior Analysis, 27*(3), 471–481.

Pierce, K., & Schreibman, L. (1995). Increasing complex social behaviors in children with autism: Effects of peer-implemented pivotal response training. *Journal of Applied Behavior Analysis, 28*(3), 285–295.

Pierce, K., & Schreibman, L. (1997). Multiple peer use of pivotal response training to increase social behaviors of classmates with autism: Results from trained and untrained peers. *Journal of Applied Behavior Analysis, 30*(1), 157–160.

Pretti-Frontczak, K., & Bricker, D. (2004). *An activity-based approach to early intervention* (3rd ed.). Baltimore, MD: Paul H. Brookes Publishing Co.

Prizant, B.M., Wetherby, A.M., Rubin, E., Laurent, A.C., & Rydell, P.J. (2006). *The SCERTS® model: A comprehensive educational approach for children with autism spectrum disorders.* Baltimore, MD: Paul H. Brookes Publishing Co.

Quill, K.A. (2000). *Do-watch-listen-say: Social and communication intervention for children with autism.* Baltimore: Paul H. Brookes Publishing Co.

Robertson, J., Green, K., Alper, S., Schloss, P.J., & Kohler, F. (2003). Using a peer-mediated intervention to facilitate children's participation in inclusive childcare activities. *Education & Treatment of Children, 26*(2), 182–197.

Rogers, S.J., & Dawson, G. (2010). *Early start Denver model for young children with autism: Promoting language, learning, and engagement.* New York: Guilford.

Rush, D.D., Shelden, M.L., & Hanft, B.E. (2003). Coaching families and colleagues: A process for collaboration in natural settings. *Infants and Young Children, 16*(1), 33–47.

Rutter, M., Bailey, A. & Lord, C. (2003). *Social Communication Questionnaire* (SCQ). Torrance, CA: Western Psychological Services.

Sansosti, F.J., & Powell-Smith, K.A. (2008). Using computer-presented Social Stories and video models to increase the social communication skills of children with high-functioning autism spectrum disorders. *Journal of Positive Behavior Interventions, 10*(3), 162–178.

Schwartz, I.S., Garfinkle, A.N., & Bauer, J. (1998). The Picture Exchange Communication System: Communicative outcomes for young children with disabilities. *Topics in Early Childhood Special Education, 18,* 144–159.

Shelden, M.L., & Rush, D.D. (2001). The ten myths about providing early intervention services. *Infants and Young Children, 14*(1), 1–13.

Skinner, B.F. (1957). *Verbal behavior.* Englewood Cliffs, NJ: Prentice Hall.

Skokut, M., Robinson, S., Openden, D., & Jimerson, S.R. (2008). Promoting the social and cognitive competence of children with autism: Interventions at school. *The California School Psychologist, 13,* 93–108.

Snell, M.E., & Gast, D.L. (1981). Applying time delay procedure to the instruction of the severely handicapped. *Journal of the Association of the Severely Handicapped, 6,* 3–14.

Sparrow, S.S., Cicchetti, D.V., & Balla, D.A. (2005). *Vineland Adaptive Behavior Scales-II* (VABS-II) (2nd ed.) Bloomington, MN: AGS Publishing/Pearson Assessments.

Spooner, F. (1984). Comparisons of backward chaining and total task presentation in training severely handicapped persons. *Education and Training in Mental Retardation, 19,* 15–22.

Stokes, T.F., & Baer, D.M. (1977). An implicit technology of generalization. *Journal of Applied Behavior Analysis, 10,* 349–367.

Sundberg, M.L. (2008). *Verbal Behavior Milestones Assessment and Placement Program.* VB-MAPP. Concord, CA: Advancements in Verbal Behavior Press.

Sundberg, M.L., & Michael, J. (2001). The benefits of Skinner's analysis of verbal behavior or children with autism. *Behavior Modification, 25,* 698–724.

Swaggart, B., et al. (1995). Using Social Stories to teach social and behavioral skills to children with autism. *Focus on Autistic Behavior, 10,* 1–16.

Thiemann, K.S., & Goldstein, H. (2001). Social Stories, written text cues, and video feedback: Effects on social communication of children with autism. *Journal of Applied Behavior Analysis, 34,* 425–446.

Thompson, T. (2011). *Individualized autism intervention for young children: Blending discrete trial and naturalistic strategies.* Baltimore, MD: Paul H. Brookes Publishing Co.

Vollmer, T.R., & Iwata, B.A. (1992). Differential reinforcement as treatment for behavior disorders: Procedural and functional variations. *Research in Developmental Disabilities, 13,* 393–417.

Wechsler, D. (2002). *Wechsler Preschool and Primary Scale of Intelligence* (WPSSI). (3rd ed). Bloomington, MN: Pearson Assessments.

Wetherby, A., & Woods, J. (2006). Early social interaction project for children with autism spectrum disorders beginning in the second year of life: A preliminary study. *Topics in Early Childhood Special Education, 26*(2), 67–82.

Wielder, S., & Greenspan, S.I. (2003). Climbing the symbolic ladder in the DIR model through floor time/interactive play. *Autism: The International Journal of Research and Practice, 7*(4), 425–435.

Wolery, M., Ault, M.J., & Doyle, P.M. (1992). *Teaching students with moderate to severe disabilities.* White Plains, NY: Longman.

Wolery, M., & Gast, D.L. (1984). Effective and efficient procedures for the transfer of stimulus control. *Topics in Early Childhood Special Education, 4,* 381–386.

Woods, J.J., & Wetherby, A.M. (2003). Early identification of and intervention for infants and toddlers who are at risk for autism spectrum disorder. *Language, Speech & Hearing Services In Schools, 34*(3), 180–193.

Woods, J.J., Wilcox, M., Friedman, M., & Murch, T. (2011). Collaborative consultation in natural environments: Strategies to enhance family-centered supports and services. *Language, Speech & Hearing Services In Schools, 42*(3), 379–392.

Zanolli, K.M., Paden, P., & Cox, K. (1997). Teaching prosocial behavior to typically developing toddlers. *Journal of Behavioral Education, 7*(3), 373–391.

Reader's Guide

· ·

CHAPTER ONE

Overview of Natural Environment Intervention

1. Many early intervention providers adamantly believe that therapeutic service delivery models are better than natural environment intervention service delivery models. What would you say to inform someone about the importance of natural environment intervention?

2. Implementing routines-based and activity-based interventions requires caregivers and early childhood teachers to take an active role in delivering interventions for young children with ASD and related disabilities. If caregivers or teachers show resistance to this responsibility, what would you say to help them recognize the value of their involvement in the delivery of interventions?

3. Think of some children with ASD that you have worked with or know personally. Describe the unique characteristics of each child in terms of social interaction, communication, behavior, and other characteristics discussed in Chapter 1.

4. Discuss the rationale for using ABA interventions within the natural environment to meet the needs of young children with ASD and other disabilities. Do you think all young children would benefit from some embedded, explicit instruction within their everyday routines?

5. What would be unique about natural environment interventions for young children with ASD in comparison with interventions for children with less significant developmental delays?

CHAPTER TWO

Understanding Applied Behavior Analysis

1. Discuss how ABA came into existence. What are its historical roots?

2. In your own words discuss the meaning of ABA. How can ABA be useful for young children within the context of their everyday routines?

3. Describe the seven dimensions of ABA and give an example to illustrate how each dimension can be addressed when designing ABA interventions in the natural environment for young children with ASD and related disabilities.

4. Describe the similarities and differences among discrete trial training (DTT), incidental teaching (IT), Pivotal Response Treatment (PRT), and applied verbal behavior (AVB).

5. The author does not recommend that early intervention providers select a specific application of ABA such as DTT, PRT, IT, or AVB as the sole intervention model for young children with ASD when implementing interventions in the natural environment. Instead, the strategies utilized within these approaches can be used in a variety of ways, along with other behavioral strategies, to develop quality ABA interventions. Why do you think the author makes this suggestion about using ABA in the natural environment?

CHAPTER THREE

Assessment for Planning ABA Interventions in the Natural Environment

1. What are the five main purposes of assessment when planning ABA interventions in the natural environment?

2. Discuss the importance of assessing the strengths and interests of young children with ASD. What strategies can you use to keep caregivers and early childhood teachers from discussions focusing on the child's limitations when you are assessing strengths and interests?

3. What are some questions you might want to add to the strengths and interests interview provided in Chapter 3?

4. Deliver the communication or social interaction assessment provided in Chapter 3 and write a summary of the child's present level of performance. Specifically include what the child can currently do independently and with support to allow an early intervention team to select developmentally appropriate goals for the child based on the detailed description.

5. Why is it important to assess the priorities of caregivers? Why do you think the author suggests doing so after the child's present levels of performance are discussed?

6. Describe the process of assessing the everyday routines of young children with ASD for purposes of planning embedded ABA interventions.

7. Chapter 3 provides a great many assessment tools. Assessing and setting goals for every domain discussed at the onset of intervention planning can be overwhelm-

ing for caregivers. How would you decide which assessments to conduct initially when working with caregivers of young children with ASD?

CHAPTER FOUR

Goal Setting for ABA Interventions in the Natural Environment

1. How can you work collaboratively with early intervention team members to set goals for ABA interventions in the natural environment for young children with ASD and related disabilities? How can you ensure that all parties are involved in the decision making, including caregivers, teachers, and related service providers?

2. The criteria for writing goals for ABA interventions stipulate that the goals must be functional, developmentally appropriate, observable, measurable, and positively stated. Practice writing goals using these criteria by writing one goal for each of the following domains: social interaction, communication, independent play skills, daily living skills, cognitive skills, and positive behavior.

3. How can you ensure that the goals selected for a child are developmentally appropriate?

4. How are goals for everyday routines different from goals that are domain-specific?

5. What is the purpose of using a routines matrix?

CHAPTER FIVE

Developing Teaching Procedures for ABA Interventions in the Natural Environment

1. How would you explain the rationale for using positive behavioral supports with young children with ASD and related disabilities as opposed to punitive consequences for challenging behavior?

2. What are the different types of positive reinforcement described in Chapter 5? Which type do you find yourself using most often? How could you increase opportunities for natural reinforcement in your work with children and families?

3. How can the use of differential reinforcement of alternative behavior reduce problem behavior?

4. What are the two different types of prompting/fading procedures? Give an example for how you would use each type when teaching a young child a new skill.

5. Embedded discrete trials can be used throughout a child's day to teach new skills. Explain what an embedded discrete trial would look like when teaching a child to request a desired item by pointing.

6. Under what circumstances would it be appropriate to select video modeling as an instructional strategy?

7. How would you go about using peer-mediated interventions to teach a young child to engage in joint play with a peer?

CHAPTER SIX

Data Collection and Analysis

1. Why is it important to collect data when implementing ABA interventions in the natural environment?

2. What type of data collection system would be the easiest for caregivers to use on a consistent basis?

3. Discuss how you would communicate with caregivers who are not collecting data on a regular basis. How might you effectively inform them of the value of doing so?

4. Discuss what should be done if the data indicate that a child is not making adequate progress on a specific objective.

5. What might you suggest if the caregivers indicate they feel their child is making progress but the data are not showing growth?

CHAPTER SEVEN

Putting It All Together

1. What role do you see yourself playing in the process of designing and implementing ABA interventions in the natural environment for young children with ASD and other disabilities?

2. What ideas do you have for providing modeling and coaching to caregivers to support them in implementing ABA interventions in the natural environment?

3. What ideas do you have for providing modeling and coaching to preschool teachers to support them in implementing ABA interventions during everyday school routines?

4. What are the different options the author shared for utilizing the information provided in this book? Do you have additional ideas for using what you have learned?

Sample Communication Skills Teaching Plans

• •

CHILD'S NAME: Sarah

DOMAIN: Communication

OBJECTIVE: Sarah will verbally request help in a calm manner independently for five consecutive days across a variety of contexts.

ROUTINES TO TARGET: Playing with toys, playing outside, meals

DATA COLLECTION PROCEDURES: Level of independence data

Explanation of data collection procedures:
4: Independent
3: Minimal prompting (time delay)
2: Moderate prompting (time delay with an outstretched hand)
1: Maximum prompting (modeling/request imitation)

TEACHING PROCEDURES:

1. When Sarah is engaged in an activity that she typically needs help with, remain in close proximity to her.

2. If Sarah begins to show signs of frustration, use most-to-least prompts to teach her how to say "help" by using the following prompting/fading sequence:

    a. Use modeling/request imitation by saying, "Do you need help?" and stressing the word *help* (put your hand out if she needs help with something she can give to you). Have Sarah imitate the word "help," and provide the help she needs.

    b. After a few trials implemented as above, begin to fade the prompt by using time delay (wait time with expectant look/body language) when she shows signs of frustration to encourage her to say "help" without a verbal prompt (still put your hand out if appropriate).

(continued)

125

    c.   Provide help if she says "help," or go back to the previous step.

    d.   Once Sarah can respond with time delay and/or an outstretched hand, fade out the use of an outstretched hand and expectant look/body language during the brief time delay to encourage independent initiations of asking for help.

    e.   Once Sarah can ask for help when an adult is in close proximity, begin to gradually increase the distance between Sarah and an adult until she can verbally request help in a calm manner even if an adult is in another room.

- -

CHILD'S NAME: Jonathan

DOMAIN: Communication

OBJECTIVE: Jonathan will request desired items using a variety of different simple sentences independently for five consecutive days.

ROUTINES TO TARGET: Playing with toys, riding in the car, meals, bath

DATA COLLECTION PROCEDURES: Level of independence data

Explanation of data collection procedures:
4: Independent
3: Minimal prompting (time delay)
2: Moderate prompting (a question was asked or a fill-in was provided)
1: Maximum prompting (modeling/request imitation)

TEACHING PROCEDURES:

1.   Use environmental arrangements to provide opportunities for Jonathan to request items from others using simple sentences. For example, hold something out of reach, place something on a shelf that is out of reach, give small amounts to provide opportunities to request more, or entice Jonathan by showing something desirable.

2.   You can also follow Jonathan's lead by using opportunities that occur naturally to teach Jonathan to request using simple sentences. If Jonathan is reaching for something, whining, grabbing, or requests an item using a one- or two-word utterance, get the item, hold it, and use time delay to encourage him to verbally request it using a simple sentence.

3.   If Jonathan uses a simple sentence to request, provide natural reinforcement by giving access to the item. Also make sure to provide social reinforcement by smiling and making a positive comment after he responds.

4. If Jonathan doesn't respond, use the following least-to-most prompts hierarchy:

   a. Use time delay (wait time with an expectant look/body language).

   b. Say "What do you want?" "What would you like?" or something similar.

   c. Use a fill-in such as "Can I have _____ ?" or "I want _____."

   d. Use modeling/request imitation by saying the sentence and having Jonathan imitate the sentence.

5. Provide positive reinforcement as indicated in Step 3 even if prompting was provided.

• •

CHILD'S NAME: Daniel

DOMAIN: Communication

OBJECTIVE: Daniel will follow at least 10 different simple one-step directions consistently.

ROUTINES TO TARGET: Playing with toys, bedtime routine, bath, meals, reading books, going for a walk

DATA COLLECTION PROCEDURES: Frequency data

Explanation of data collection procedures:
When Daniel follows a simple one-step direction without prompts, write it down. Each time he follows that direction without prompts, put a tally mark next to it. Once Daniel has five tally marks next to a direction, include that direction in a frequency count of simple one-step directions he can follow. Once a week, graph the number of directions he can follow consistently (at least five tally marks = consistent).

TEACHING PROCEDURES:

1. Within a naturally occurring routine, give Daniel a simple one-step direction to follow (e.g. "Put your clothes in the hamper," "Put the book back," "Put the wrapper in the garbage.").

2. If he follows the direction independently, provide positive reinforcement.

3. If he doesn't follow the direction, use the following least-to-most prompts hierarchy:

   a. Restate the direction and use time delay.

   b. Use a gesture/point.

(continued)

    c. Use modeling/request imitation or help him get started, and then have him finish the direction independently.

    d. Provide gentle physical assistance throughout.

4. Once he responds (even with prompting), use positive reinforcement.

CHILD'S NAME: Jessica

DOMAIN: Communication

OBJECTIVE: Jessica will imitate "no" when she doesn't want something, using a verbal approximation or shaking her head independently for five consecutive days.

ROUTINES TO TARGET: Meals, playing with toys, dressing

DATA COLLECTION PROCEDURES: Level of independence data

Explanation of data collection procedures:
4: Independent
3: Minimal prompting (Make your mouth look like you are going to say "no," use a gesture/sign, begin to shake your head.)
2: Moderate prompting (Shake your head in an exaggerated manner and say "no" multiple times.)
1: Maximum prompting (Say "no," and prompt Jessica to touch a picture symbol indicating "no.")

TEACHING PROCEDURES:

1. When Jessica indicates that she doesn't want something by turning away or pushing an item away, before taking it away, say, "Do you want this?" or "Do you want it?" or "Do you want the _____?"

2. If she says "no" (or an approximation) or shakes her head, provide reinforcement by taking away the item.

3. If she doesn't say "no" (or an approximation) or shake her head, use the following least-to-most prompts hierarchy:

    a. Make your mouth look like you are going to say "no."

    b. Use a sign or gesture to show "no" or shake your head.

    c. Shake your head in an exaggerated manner and say "no" multiple times.

    d. Say "no," and prompt her to touch a picture symbol indicating "no."

4. Once Jessica responds (even with prompting) use reinforcement by taking away the item.

Sample Social Interaction Skills Teaching Plans

. . . .

CHILD'S NAME: Christopher

DOMAIN: Social interaction

OBJECTIVE: Christopher will imitate actions with a variety of toys during play activities independently for five consecutive days.

ROUTINES TO TARGET: Playing with toys (farmhouse, trains, cars, blocks, pretend kitchen), bath, visiting a friend's house

DATA COLLECTION PROCEDURES: Level of independence data

Explanation of data collection procedures:
4: Independent
3: Minimal prompting (modeling/request imitation, time delay, verbal prompt, light tap)
2: Moderate prompting (help him get started, then fade out assistance quickly)
1: Maximum prompting (gentle physical assistance throughout)

TEACHING PROCEDURES:

Implement the following procedures during interest-based play activities:

1. Follow Christopher's lead by joining him in a play activity.

2. After about 30 seconds of playing alongside him, dramatically demonstrate an action with toys.

3. If Christopher imitates, provide positive reinforcement.

4. If he doesn't imitate the action, use the following least-to-most prompts hierarchy:

   a. Use modeling/request imitation by repeating the action and using time delay.

(continued)

b.   Say something such as, "Now you do it" or "It's your turn."

c.   Lightly tap him.

d.   Help him get started, then fade out assistance quickly.

e.   Provide gentle physical assistance throughout.

5.   Once Christopher responds (even with prompting), use positive reinforcement.

6.   Provide multiple opportunities each day during a variety of play activities.

Note: The objective is to get Christopher to watch you and do what you are doing, not to have him memorize which actions go with particular toys, so be sure to use many different toys and actions. Make changes to the actions if you think he is simply memorizing the routine with a particular toy.

• •

CHILD'S NAME: Amy

DOMAIN: Social interaction

OBJECTIVE: Amy will verbally or nonverbally initiate play with another peer during recess or centers at least once each day independently

ROUTINES TO TARGET: Centers, recess

DATA COLLECTION PROCEDURES: Yes/no data

Explanation of data collection procedures:
Yes: Amy initiated play with a peer at least once independently.
No: Amy did not initiate play with a peer or needed prompting to do so.

TEACHING PROCEDURES:

1.   Introduce a Social Story to teach Amy different ways to initiate play, and do this:

a.   Have her view the social story on the computer (a teacher can read it to her or audio can be embedded so she can view it independently).

b.   After she views the story, ask her to retell what she learned.

c.   Follow up with additional comprehension questions to ensure understanding. (If she is unable to answer any of the questions, reread parts of the Social Story and ask the questions again. Increase prompts if necessary.)

    d. Each day, have her view the social story immediately before recess and/or centers.

2. If Amy initiates play with a peer, provide positive reinforcement after the children are finished playing (e.g. "I love how you asked to play with Justin in the water center!").

3. Use peer-mediated interventions to teach peers to respond positively to Amy's initiations.

4. If Amy does not initiate play, use the following least-to-most prompts hierarchy:

    a. Provide a visual prompt (this can be a small picture of the cover of the social story or a picture of a child requesting to play with another child).

    b. Provide a gestural prompt (point to children playing).

    c. Provide a verbal prompt (e.g. "It's time to ask a friend to play.").

    d. Use modeling/request imitation (e.g. provide the model "Can I play too?" and have Amy imitate).

5. Be sure to provide positive reinforcement even if Amy needed prompts to initiate play.

Note: You can use video self-modeling by embedding a short video clip of Amy initiating play with a peer into the social story using PowerPoint.

• •

CHILD'S NAME: Ben

DOMAIN: Social interaction

OBJECTIVE: Ben will engage in reciprocal verbal and/or nonverbal interactions with peers during a variety of interest-based activities for two minutes independently.

ROUTINES TO TARGET: Centers, recess, visiting friends' houses, playing with toys with siblings or friends, playing outside with siblings or friends, bathtime with sibling

DATA COLLECTION PROCEDURES: Level of independence data

Explanation of data collection procedures:
4: Independent
3: Minimal prompting: Needed very little adult facilitation
2: Moderate prompting: Needed adult facilitation for most of the duration
1: Maximum prompting: Needed adult facilitation for the majority of the duration

---

(continued)

TEACHING PROCEDURES:

1. Begin the activity by having a peer follow Ben's lead or by having the peer initiate play with Ben using interest-based materials.

2. As the peer begins interacting with Ben, use peer-mediated interventions to teach the peer to make comments, ask questions, or give directions throughout the play period and use time delay (pause with an expectant look/body language) to encourage Ben to respond.

3. If Ben doesn't respond to the peer, use adult facilitation as needed by using prompting/fading procedures to provide the necessary supports for Ben to engage with the peer. The prompts can be gestural, visual, verbal, or physical, but be sure to fade out any prompts being used as soon as possible.

4. Encourage the peer to provide positive reinforcements throughout the play period when Ben responds appropriately by smiling and making positive comments.

• •

CHILD'S NAME: Luke

DOMAIN: Social interaction

OBJECTIVE: Luke will allow an adult or peer to engage in parallel play during preferred activities, remaining calm, for five consecutive days.

ROUTINES TO TARGET: Playing with toys, playing in the sandbox, playing at the water table, playing on the slide at the playground

DATA COLLECTION PROCEDURES: Individualized rating scale

Explanation of data collection procedures:
4: Remained calm when an adult or peer engaged in parallel play.
3: Got mildly upset (whined, complained) when an adult or peer engaged in parallel play.
2: Cried or yelled when an adult or peer engaged in parallel play.
1: Engaged in aggression or ran away when an adult or peer engaged in parallel play.

TEACHING PROCEDURES:

1. When Luke is engaged in a preferred activity, follow his lead by joining him.

2. Sit in close proximity to Luke. If he has a strong aversion to your proximity, use shaping by sitting farther away and gradually decreasing the distance as he gets comfortable with your presence.

3. If Luke displays challenging behaviors such as moving away, yelling, crying, or aggressive acts, ignore the challenging behavior and continue playing next to him. You may need to provide physical guidance to keep him in the same area as you. Be sure to fade out the physical guidance, however, to teach him to stay in the area without support.

4. Once Luke is able to stay in the same area, make positive comments while playing alongside him such as "I am building a tower," or "I like what you are building." You can also use contingent imitation by imitating what he is doing.

5. Provide positive reinforcement when Luke allows you to engage in parallel play without engaging in challenging behaviors.

6. If a peer is playing, use peer-mediated interventions by teaching the peer the procedures in Steps 1 through 5. However, if Luke needs physical prompting, do not allow a peer to provide that support.

Sample Independent Play and Daily Living Skills Teaching Plans

• •

CHILD'S NAME: Sean

DOMAIN: Daily living skills

OBJECTIVE: Sean will wash his hands, completing 100% of the steps independently.

ROUTINES TO TARGET: Before and after meals, after playing outside

DATA COLLECTION PROCEDURES: Percentage data

Explanation of data collection procedures:
Indicate how many of the seven steps of the hand washing procedure Sean completes independently and divide by seven to get a percentage.

TEACHING PROCEDURES:

1. Use task analysis/chaining to teach Sean to perform the hand washing steps below:

   a. Turn the water on.

   b. Run hands under the water.

   c. Put soap on hands.

   d. Rub hands together to make suds.

   e. Rinse soap off hands.

   f. Turn off the water.

   g. Dry hands with a towel.

2. Use total task presentation by having Sean complete the steps that are easiest for him and gradually adding on the more difficult steps of the task until Sean is able to complete the entire task independently. Create a visual schedule of the steps for Sean to follow.

(continued)

3. Use least-to-most prompts to assist Sean in learning the steps of the task using the following hierarchy:

    a. Use modeling/request imitation.

    b. Use gestural prompts.

    c. Use verbal prompts.

    d. Provide gentle physical assistance.

4. Provide positive reinforcement at the completion of the task. While you can provide positive reinforcement after Sean completes each step of the task, this may cause him to stop engaging in the task. Therefore, if possible, delay positive reinforcement until the task is complete.

• •

CHILD'S NAME: Lily

DOMAIN: Independent play skills

OBJECTIVE: Lily will play with a variety of age-appropriate toys independently for at least five minutes at a time.

ROUTINES TO TARGET: Playing with toys, bathtime, playing outside, riding in the car, visiting a friend's house, waiting for food at a restaurant

DATA COLLECTION PROCEDURES: Level of independence data

Explanation of data collection procedures:
4: Independent
3: Minimal prompting: Needed 1 or 2 prompts to play independently
2: Moderate prompting: Needed 3 or 4 prompts to play independently
1: Maximum prompting: Needed ongoing prompts to play independently

---

TEACHING PROCEDURES:

1. Consider Lily's strengths and interests when selecting toys for independent play.

2. To teach Lily to play independently, you will first need to facilitate the play. Provide least-to-most prompts to keep Lily focused on the play activity using the following hierarchy:

    a. Use modeling/request imitation.

    b. Use gestural prompts.

    c. Use verbal prompts.

    d. Use gentle physical assistance.

3. Once Lily can play with the toy appropriately, begin to fade out your presence to teach her to play independently. You may need to come in and out of the play activity to keep her engaged, but continually work on fading yourself out.

4. Provide positive reinforcement after the play period is over, even if Lily needed prompting to engage.

* *

CHILD'S NAME: Jacob

DOMAIN: Daily living skills

OBJECTIVE: Jacob will eat a variety of foods with a spoon independently for five consecutive days.

ROUTINES TO TARGET: Snacks, meals

DATA COLLECTION PROCEDURES: Level of independence data

Explanation of data collection procedures:
4: Independent
3: Minimal prompting (verbal prompts, gestures, light taps)
2: Moderate prompting (physical assistance needed often)
1: Maximum prompting (physical assistance needed throughout)

TEACHING PROCEDURES:

1. Provide foods that Jacob prefers that are easy to eat with a spoon. It is actually easier to start with solid foods if he does not like getting messy.

2. Put the food in a bowl with a spoon. If Jacob independently uses the spoon, provide positive reinforcement.

3. If Jacob begins to eat with his hands, use the following least-to-most prompts hierarchy:

    a. Point to the spoon.

    b. Give a verbal prompt such as "Eat with your spoon."

    c. Put the spoon in his hand.

    d. Lightly tap his hand.

    e. Provide some physical assistance, but then take it away ASAP.

    f. Gently guide his hand with the spoon to his mouth.

4. Each time Jacob uses the spoon (even with prompting), provide positive reinforcement.

(continued)

5. Once Jacob can eat solid foods with a spoon, move on to foods like yogurt and pudding.

· ·

CHILD'S NAME: Haley

DOMAIN: Daily living skills

OBJECTIVE: Haley will initiate using the bathroom multiple times each day and stay dry in between visits to the bathroom.

ROUTINES TO TARGET: After waking up, before meals, after meals, before playing with toys, while playing with toys, after playing with toys, before bath, before bedtime, preschool

DATA COLLECTION PROCEDURES: Yes/no data

Explanation of data collection procedures:
Yes: Haley initiated using the bathroom multiple times in the day and stayed dry.
No: Haley did not initiate using the bathroom and/or did not stay dry.

TEACHING PROCEDURES:

1. Teach Haley to initiate using the bathroom by pointing to a picture symbol for the bathroom.

2. Embed discrete trials to teach Haley how to initiate using the bathroom right before she would typically need to go to the bathroom using the following procedure:

    a. Antecedent: Place the bathroom picture symbol in close proximity to Haley.

    b. Prompt: Point to the picture symbol (if necessary, put your hand out or provide gentle physical assistance).

    c. Behavior: Haley points to the picture symbol to initiate using the bathroom.

    d. Consequence: Smile and say something such as "Great job telling me you have to go to the bathroom! Let's go!" After Haley goes to the bathroom, provide additional positive reinforcement.

3. Once Haley is able to initiate using the picture symbol during discrete trials, fade out the prompt of pointing to the picture symbol. Once she can initiate without that prompt, fade out the antecedent of placing the picture symbol in close proximity. Choose a set location for the picture symbol to be located so Haley can get it when she needs to go to the bathroom.

Sample Cognitive Skills Teaching Plans

· ·

CHILD'S NAME: Michael

DOMAIN: Cognitive skills

OBJECTIVE: Michael will receptively identify the following body parts: head, feet, eyes, with 100% accuracy.

ROUTINES TO TARGET: Dressing, bathtime, playing tickle games/wrestling with Dad

DATA COLLECTION PROCEDURES: Percentage data

> **Explanation of data collection procedures:**
> Indicate correct for all unprompted accurate responses. Indicate incorrect for all prompted or inaccurate responses. Divide the total number of correct responses by the number of opportunities to get a percentage.

TEACHING PROCEDURES:

1. Ask Michael a question such as "Where are your feet?" or say something such as "Touch your feet."

2. If Michael points to the correct body part, provide positive reinforcement.

3. If Michael does not point to the correct body part, use the following least-to-most prompts hierarchy:

   a. Restate the request and use time delay (wait with an expectant look).

   b. Use modeling/request imitation by pointing to the correct body part on Michael or yourself and then encourage him to do the same.

   c. Lightly tap his arm to get him started.

   d. Use gentle physical guidance.

4. Provide positive reinforcement even if Michael responded with a prompt(s).

(continued)

CHILD'S NAME: Sam

DOMAIN: Cognitive skills

OBJECTIVE: Sam will receptively identify basic colors when given a field of two with 100% accuracy for five consecutive days.

ROUTINES TO TARGET: Playing with toys, bathtime, reading books

DATA COLLECTION PROCEDURES: Percentage data

Explanation of data collection procedures:
Indicate correct for all unprompted accurate responses. Indicate incorrect for all prompted or inaccurate responses. Divide the total number of correct responses by the number of opportunities to get a percentage.

TEACHING PROCEDURES:

1. Present two colors to Sam by holding them at eye level using flash cards, puzzle pieces, objects from toys, or any other interest-based materials. It may be helpful to pair this with something Sam enjoys (e.g. Use shapes from the shape sorter, and present a trial before Sam puts a shape in the shape sorter.).

2. Use embedded discrete trials with the following procedures:

   a. Antecedent: Hold up two colors and ask Sam to get the indicated color. Vary your directions by saying things such as "Which one's blue?" "Find green," "Touch red," and so on.

   b. Prompt: You can move both colors closer to encourage Sam to respond, you can move only the correct color closer, you can use modeling/request imitation, or you can provide gentle physical assistance.

   c. Behavior: Sam indicates the correct color.

   d. Consequence: Positive reinforcement.

3. Be sure to fade out the prompts being used until Sam can respond correctly with no prompts at all.

CHILD'S NAME: Brittany

DOMAIN: Cognitive skills

OBJECTIVE: Brittany will engage in book sharing with an adult by sitting face-to-face and allowing the adult to hold the book and turn the pages for five consecutive days.

ROUTINES TO TARGET: Reading books before bedtime, during playing with toys routines, before/after meals, before/after videos

DATA COLLECTION PROCEDURES: Individualized rating scale

Explanation of data collection procedures:
4: Engaged in book sharing as indicated for the entire book.
3: Engaged in book sharing as indicated for the majority of the book.
2: Engaged in book sharing as indicated for about half of the book.
1: Engaged in book sharing as indicated for a small portion of the book.

TEACHING PROCEDURES:

1. Allow Brittany to select a book, given a choice of two books. Use prompting/fading procedures if necessary to teach her to point to a book.

2. Attempt to sit face-to-face with Brittany and hold the book while you read it to her. If she tries to run away or has significant behavioral challenges, have her sit in your lap while you hold the book and read it. Use shaping to gradually get her to be able to sit face-to-face.

3. To ease Brittany's frustration or anxiety, do not actually read all of the words on the page at first. Just quickly say something about the picture and then turn the page.

4. Another way to ease her frustration or anxiety is to allow her to turn the pages. Say, "Turn the page," when you are done with the page. Brittany should only be allowed to turn the page after you say so.

5. Once Brittany is able to sit calmly, you can gradually increase the complexity of the language you are using or actually read the words on the page.

(continued)

CHILD'S NAME: Lauren

DOMAIN: Cognitive skills

OBJECTIVE: Lauren will receptively identify common objects given a field of two with accuracy for all or most learning opportunities for five consecutive days.

ROUTINES TO TARGET: Playing with toys, bathtime, meals, reading books

DATA COLLECTION PROCEDURES: Individualized rating scale

Explanation of data collection procedures:
4: Receptively identified all or most objects throughout the day.
3: Receptively identified more than half of the objects throughout the day.
2: Receptively identified about half of the objects throughout the day.
1: Receptively identified less than half of the objects throughout the day.
0: Receptively identified very few or none of the objects throughout the day.

TEACHING PROCEDURES:

1. Use interest-based materials such as puzzles, farm animal figurines, pictures of objects, and books, and use embedded discrete trials with the following procedures:

   a. Antecedent: Hold up two items and ask Lauren to identify a given item by saying something such as "Where is the pig?" or "Get the pig."

   b. Prompt: You can move both objects or pictures closer to encourage Lauren to respond, you can move only the correct item closer, you can use modeling/request imitation, or you can provide gentle physical assistance.

   c. Behavior: Lauren indicates the correct object.

   d. Consequence: Positive reinforcement

2. Be sure to fade out the prompts being used until Lauren can respond correctly with no prompts at all.

Sample Positive Behaviors Teaching Plans

- -

CHILD'S NAME: Evan

DOMAIN: Positive behaviors

OBJECTIVE: Evan will remain seated in his chair at the kitchen table until he is finished with his food, for five consecutive days.

ROUTINES TO TARGET: Meals, snacks

DATA COLLECTION PROCEDURES: Yes/no data

> **Explanation of data collection procedures:**
> Yes: Evan stayed in his chair during all meals and snacks throughout the day.
> No: Evan did not stay in his chair during the meals and snacks throughout the day or needed prompts to do so.

TEACHING PROCEDURES:

1. Use video self-modeling to teach Evan the expectation of sitting in the chair to eat meals. Show Evan the video prior to each meal/snack.

2. While Evan is sitting in his chair, provide positive reinforcement.

3. If Evan gets out of his chair, use the following most-to-least prompts hierarchy immediately:

    a. Gently pick Evan up and put him back in his chair.

    b. Block Evan and point to his chair.

    c. Lightly tap his arm to get him started.

    d. Give a verbal prompt such as "Go back to your chair."

4. Provide positive reinforcement when Evan gets back in his chair.

Note: At no time should Evan have access to food when he is not in his chair.

(continued)

CHILD'S NAME: Nathan

DOMAIN: Positive behaviors

OBJECTIVE: Nathan will accept a change in his daily routine, remaining calm when the change is introduced, for five consecutive days.

ROUTINES TO TARGET: Riding in the car, meals, bathtime, bedtime routine

DATA COLLECTION PROCEDURES: Individualized rating scale

Explanation of data collection procedures:
4: Nathan remained calm when changes were initiated.
3: Nathan displayed mild discomfort when changes were initiated (e.g. brief whining, verbal complaints).
2: Nathan cried or yelled when changes were initiated.
1: Nathan engaged in aggressive behaviors (hitting, kicking, biting, scratching) when changes were initiated.

TEACHING PROCEDURES:

1. Begin by initiating changes in a routine that Nathan would consider desirable changes (e.g. instead of taking a shower, Nathan can take a bath and play.).

2. Before the change is initiated, use priming by letting Nathan know about the change that is going to take place (e.g. Say, "Tonight you will get to take a bath instead of shower!").

3. If Nathan remains calm when the change is initiated or displays mild discomfort, provide positive reinforcement.

4. If Nathan engages in challenging behaviors, ignore the challenging behaviors and positively reinforce Nathan when he calms down.

5. Once Nathan is able to remain calm during desirable changes, initiate changes that he would not necessarily consider desirable but would not consider extremely undesirable. Introduce undesirable changes after Nathan can remain calm during changes that are neither desirable nor extremely undesirable.

CHILD'S NAME: Robert

DOMAIN: Positive behaviors

OBJECTIVE: Robert will pet the dog gently for 5 consecutive days.

ROUTINES TO TARGET: Playing with toys, playing outside, bedtime routine

DATA COLLECTION PROCEDURES: Yes/no data

Explanation of data collection procedures:
Yes: Robert petted the dog nicely throughout the day.
No: Robert did not pet the dog nicely or needed reminders to pet the dog nicely throughout the day.

TEACHING PROCEDURES:

1. Use modeling/request imitation to teach Robert how to gently pet the dog.

2. If Robert does not imitate the model or acts aggressively toward the dog, use most-to-least prompts to correct the behavior, using the following hierarchy:

   a. Provide gentle physical assistance.

   b. Provide gentle physical assistance and then release to allow Robert to continue petting nicely.

   c. Use a verbal prompt (e.g. "Pet her nicely.").

3. Provide positive reinforcement each time Robert pets the dog nicely, with or without prompts.

CHILD'S NAME: Tara

DOMAIN: Positive behaviors

OBJECTIVE: Tara will point to what she wants, remaining calm until the item is given to her, for five consecutive days.

ROUTINES TO TARGET: Playing with toys, bathtime, meals, playing outside

DATA COLLECTION PROCEDURES: Yes/no data

(continued)

> **Explanation of data collection procedures:**
> Yes: Tara independently pointed to the things she wanted throughout the day and remained calm until the items were given to her.
> No: Tara did not point to the things she wanted throughout the day or needed prompting to do so.

TEACHING PROCEDURES:

1. Use environmental arrangements to provide opportunities for Tara to request items from others. For example, hold something out of reach, place something on a shelf that is out of reach, give small amounts to provide opportunities to request more, or entice her by showing something desirable.

2. You can also follow Tara's lead by using opportunities that occur naturally to teach her to make a request. If Tara is reaching for something, whining, grabbing, crying, or yelling, get the item, hold it, and use time delay to encourage her to request it by pointing.

3. If Tara points, provide reinforcement by giving access to the item. Also make sure you provide social reinforcement by smiling and making a positive comment after she points.

4. If Tara doesn't point, use least-to-most prompts using the following prompt hierarchy:

   a. Move the item closer to Tara.

   b. Say something such as "Point" or "Do you want this?"

   c. Use modeling/request imitation.

   d. Provide gentle physical guidance.

5. Give positive reinforcement even if Tara needed prompts to point.

Note: Use shaping by first reinforcing Tara if she points, even if she is still complaining or crying. Eventually only reinforce Tara when she points and waits calmly for the item.

Sample Intervention Plans for Targeted Routines

· ·

CHILD'S NAME: Rebecca

ROUTINE: Playing in the backyard

	Goals	Behavioral strategies
Communication	1. Rebecca will say "up" to go up the stairs. 2. Rebecca will fill in words for repetitive phrases such as "1, 2, ____." and "Ready, set, ____."	Time delay Embedded discrete trials
Social interaction	Rebecca will roll a ball back and forth with a partner from approximately 3 feet away.	Prompting/fading procedures Positive reinforcement
Independence	Rebecca will fill up a bucket with sand using a shovel.	Modeling/request imitation Positive reinforcement
Cognition	Rebecca will count to ten while swinging.	Modeling/request imitation Time delay Positive reinforcement
Positive behaviors	Rebecca will say "out" to request to go outside (instead of crying or yelling).	Modeling/request imitation Positive reinforcement

CHILD'S NAME: Jared

ROUTINE: Snacks/meals

	Goals	Behavioral strategies
Communication	1. Jared will use simple sentences to request desired food and drink items. 2. Jared will respond to comments and questions from his parents.	Time delay Prompting/fading procedures Positive reinforcement
Social interaction	Jared will initiate at least one interaction with a family member during each meal.	Priming Prompting/fading procedures Positive reinforcement
Independence	Jared will eat with a fork or a spoon without reminders.	Prompting/fading procedures Positive reinforcement
Cognition	NA	
Positive behaviors	NA	

CHILD'S NAME: Blake

ROUTINE: Reading books

	Goals	Behavioral strategies
Communication	Blake will narrate a story by looking at the pictures, using simple sentences.	Prompting/fading procedures Positive reinforcement
Social interaction	Blake will initiate interactions with the person sharing a book with him by asking questions or making comments.	Prompting/fading procedures Positive reinforcement

(continued)

	Goals	Behavioral strategies
Independence	NA	
Cognition	Blake will listen to a story read aloud and answer simple literal questions during the story.	Prompting/fading procedures Positive reinforcement
Positive behaviors	NA	

CHILD'S NAME: Ashley

ROUTINE: Riding in the car

	Goals	Behavioral strategies
Communication	Ashley will request songs, using at least one-word utterances.	Embedded discrete trials
Social interaction	Ashley will imitate her sister's dance movements.	Peer-mediated interventions Modeling/request imitation Positive reinforcement
Independence	Ashley will climb in and out of her car seat independently.	Prompting/fading procedures Positive reinforcement
Cognition	Ashley will recite the ABCs.	Modeling/request imitation Time delay Positive reinforcement
Positive behaviors	Ashley will remain buckled in her car seat during car rides.	Priming Positive reinforcement

G

Blank Forms for Assessment, Goal Setting, and Data Collection

· ·

Assessing Strengths and Interests: Caregiver Interview
Preference Assessment Recording Form
Assessing Communication Skills
Assessing Social Interaction Skills
Assessing Social Skills
Assessing Independent Play Skills
Assessing Daily Living Skills
Assessing Cognitive Skills
Assessment of Challenging Behaviors
Assessing Caregiver Priorities
Assessment of Everyday Routines and Activities
Ecological Assessment for Everyday Routines
ABA Activity-Based Instruction Matrix
Goals for Targeted Routine
ABA Teaching Plan Template
Intervention Plan for Targeted Routine
Percentage Correct Data Sheet
Level of Independence Data Sheet
Frequency Data Sheet
Yes/No Data Collection Sheet

Assessing Strengths and
Interests: Caregiver Interview

Date	Child's name	Interviewer	Caregiver responding

Opening statement	Caregiver response
Tell me about your child's strengths and interests.	

Additional probing questions	Caregiver response
What makes your child happy?	
How does your child prefer to spend his or her time?	
What are your child's favorite toys or activities?	
In what areas does your child excel?	
What about your child makes you proud?	

Additional probing questions	Caregiver response
Who does your child like to spend time with?	
What are your child's favorite times of the day?	
What keeps your child's attention?	
What are your child's favorite places?	
What would your child never want to give up?	
What are your child's favorite snacks, meals, and drinks?	
Assessing aversions and fears	**Caregiver response**
Does your child have any intense aversions or fears?	

Preference Assessment
Recording Form

Child's name: _____

Date/activity	Choice 1	Choice 2	Selection

Assessing Communication Skills

Child's name: _____ Caregiver interviewed: _____ Date: _____

Question	Information gathered from interview(s)	Information gathered from direct observation
How does your child express wants and needs? (e.g. grabbing, pulling, pushing, crying/whining, pointing, reaching, eye contact, facial expressions, sounds, words)		
How does your child express frustration or anger? (e.g. crying, hitting, spitting, walking away, eye contact, sounds, words)		
What does your child do to gain your attention? (e.g. cry, whine, reach for you, climb on you, make sounds, say words, make eye contact, use facial expressions)		
What types of directions can your child follow? (e.g. one-step simple, one-step complex, two-step simple, two-step complex, multistep)		
What sounds does your child babble, if any?		

Question	Information gathered from interview(s)	Information gathered from direct observation
Describe your child's ability to imitate verbalizations. (e.g. sounds, words, phrases, sentences)		
What items can your child identify receptively by pointing, touching, giving, or getting, if any? (with books, objects, flash cards, puzzle pieces, etc.)		
How does your child indicate when he doesn't want something? (e.g. shake head, move away, cry, say no)		
How does your child respond to the question, "Do you want _____?" (e.g. take the item, move away, cry, nod head, shake head, say yes/no)		
How does your child let you know that something is enjoyable? (e.g. smiling, pointing, nodding, showing, eye contact, sounds, words)		
How does your child communicate to initiate social interactions with peers? (e.g. eye contact, facial expressions, body language, proximity, gestures, sounds, words)		

Additional questions for children who are verbal	Information gathered from interview(s)	Information gathered from direct observation
What types of questions can your child answer, if any? (e.g. Simple questions such as "What is this?" Questions about present activities, past events, future events, age-appropriate common knowledge, emotions/feelings)		
What types of questions can your child ask, if any? (e.g. Asking what something is, where something is, or when something is going to occur. Questions to find out what someone else is thinking, how someone else is feeling, or why something happened)		
What types of comments does your child respond to, if any? (e.g. Comments during present activities, conversational comments)		
What types of comments does your child initiate, if any? (e.g. Comments to share enjoyment, information, opinions, or wishes)		
To what extent can your child engage in a conversation? (e.g. number of back-and-forth exchanges, preferred/non-preferred topics, with peers/adults, appropriately initiate and end conversations)		

Assessing Social Interaction Skills

Child's name: _____ Caregiver interviewed: _____ Date: _____

Describe your child's ability to...	Information gathered from interviews	Information gathered from direct observation
Allow others to join play 1. *Allow an adult or peer to engage in parallel play during a preferred activity* 2. *Allow two or more peers to engage in parallel play during a preferred activity*		
Respond to joint attention bids from others 1. *Respond to a point with a verbal request to look* 2. *Respond to a verbal request to look* 3. *Respond to a nonverbal play initiation* 4. *Respond to a verbal play initiation* 5. *Give a turn at the request of a peer or adult*		
Maintain joint attention across a variety of activities 1. *Imitate the actions of others* 2. *Respond to requests or directions during ongoing activities* 3. *Respond to questions during ongoing activities* 4. *Respond to comments during ongoing activities* 5. *Make requests or give directions during ongoing activities*		

Describe your child's ability to…	Information gathered from interviews	Information gathered from direct observation
6. Make comments during ongoing activities 7. Ask questions during ongoing activities 8. Offer toys or materials to a peer or adult during ongoing activities 9. Maintain joint attention for a specified period of time 10. Engage in long chains of reciprocal interactions for a specified period of time		
Initiate joint attention 1. Imitate a peer or adult during play activities 2. Ask for a turn and remain in close proximity while taking a turn 3. Point to something and make eye contact to share information/enjoyment 4. Make a comment to share information/ enjoyment 5. Ask a question about something in the environment 6. Initiate play by joining an ongoing play activity with peers 7. Initiate play with a verbal request		

Assessing Social Skills

Child's name: _____ Caregiver interviewed: _____ Date: _____

Skill	Independent	Minimal prompting	Moderate prompting	Maximum prompting
Shares materials during parallel play				
Shares materials during joint play				
Responds when others offer a turn				
Offers a turn to others				
Maintains attention while waiting for a turn				
Offers help to others				
Accepts help from others				
Empathizes with the feelings of others				
Uses appropriate voice volume				
Uses appropriate space with a social partner				
Responds to greetings				
Initiates greetings				
Uses appropriate eye contact when interacting with others				
Gives compliments to others				
Receives compliments positively				
Responds appropriately to facial expressions of others				
Responds appropriately to body language of others				
Appropriately responds when others are in the way				
Other:				
Other:				
Other:				
Other:				

Assessing Independent Play Skills

Child's name: _____ Caregiver interviewed: _____ Date: _____

Question	Caregiver response	Direct observation
1. List all of the different activities your child engages in during independent play.		
2. Approximately how long does your child engage in independent play without needing adult support?		
3. Describe any stereotypic or inappropriate behaviors your child engages in during independent play.		

Assessing Daily Living Skills

Child's name: _____ Caregiver interviewed: _____ Date: _____

Skill	Independent	Minimal prompting	Moderate prompting	Maximum prompting	No opportunity
Eats finger foods					
Eats using a fork					
Eats using a spoon					
Drinks with a straw					
Drinks from a cup					
Washes hands					
Washes face					
Brushes teeth					
Brushes hair					
Uses the toilet					
Washes body					
Washes hair					
Gets dressed					
Gets undressed					
Other:					
Other:					
Other:					
Other:					

Assessing Cognitive Skills

Child's name: _____ Caregiver interviewed: _____ Date: _____

Problem-solving skills	Mastery	Near mastery	Developing	Has not been introduced	Notes
Uses a shape sorter					
Stacks rings					
Nests cups					
Completes peg puzzles					
Completes 24-piece puzzles					
Creates structures with blocks or other manipulative toys					
Matches (objects, shapes, colors)					
Sorts objects, colors, shapes					

Vocabulary	Mastery	Near mastery	Developing	Has not been introduced	Notes
Receptive identification of common objects (3D/2D; field of 2, 3, many)					
Expressive identification of common objects (3D/2D)					
Receptive identification of body parts					

Vocabulary *(continued)*	**Mastery**	**Near mastery**	**Developing**	**Has not been introduced**	**Notes**
Expressive identification of body parts					
Receptive identification of verbs (field of 2, 3, many)					
Expressive identification of verbs					
Receptive color identification (field of 2, 3, many)					
Expressive color identification					
Receptive shape identification (field of 2, 3, many)					
Expressive shape identification					

Literacy skills	**Mastery**	**Near mastery**	**Developing**	**Has not been introduced**	**Notes**
Recites the alphabet					
Matches letters (uppercase, lowercase, uppercase and lowercase)					
Receptive identification of uppercase letters (field of 2, 3, many)					

Literacy skills *(continued)*	Mastery	Near mastery	Developing	Has not been introduced	Notes
Expressive identification of upper-case letters					
Receptive identification of lowercase letters (field of 2, 3, many)					
Expressive identification of lowercase letters					
"Reads" a book independently by turning the pages one at a time from the beginning to the end, holding the book right side up					
Demonstrates concept of print by tracking words with a pointer finger from left to right					
Attends while being read to					
Responds to questions/comments about pictures in a book					
Narrates a story by looking at the pictures					
"Reads" by using memory to recite the story					

Literacy skills *(continued)*	Mastery	Near mastery	Developing	Has not been introduced	Notes
Predicts what a book will be about by looking at the cover and/or hearing the title					
Retells a story					
Responds to literal questions about a story (during and after the story)					
Responds to inferential questions about a story (during and after the story)					
Reads fluently (pre-primer/primer levels)					

Math skills	Mastery	Near mastery	Developing	Has not been introduced	Notes
Rote counts to 10					
Rote counts to 20					
Matches numbers					
Receptive identification of numbers 0–10 (field of 2, 3, many)					
Expressive identification of numbers 0–10					

Math skills *(continued)*	Mastery	Near mastery	Developing	Has not been introduced	Notes
Receptive identification of numbers 11–20 (field of 2, 3, many)					
Expressive identification of numbers 11–20					
One-to-one correspondence up to 10					
One-to-one correspondence up to 20					
Matches sets of objects to a number (objects and pictures)					
Identifies more and less					
Identifies all, some, and none					
Puts numbers in sequential order					
Adds 1D + 1D with manipulatives					

Assessment of Challenging Behaviors

Child's name: _____ Caregiver interviewed: _____ Date: _____

List the challenging behaviors that your child displays.	
Which behavior(s) listed would you like to target for intervention?	

For each behavior that the caregivers would like to target for intervention, complete the information below:

Question	Caregiver response
1. When, where, and with whom is the behavior most or least likely to occur?	
2. What typically happens right before and right after the behavior?	
3. What purpose do you think the behavior serves for your child?	
4. What may be an appropriate replacement behavior that can serve the same purpose?	
5. What changes may need to be made within the environment to decrease the occurrence of the challenging behavior?	
6. How might the behavior of others (e.g. caregivers, siblings, peers) need to be changed to decrease the occurrence of the challenging behavior?	

Assessing Caregiver Priorities

Child's name: _____ Caregiver interviewed: _____ Date: _____

Domain	Caregiver priorities
Communication	1. 2. 3.
Social interaction/social skills	1. 2. 3.
Independent play skills	1. 2. 3.
Daily living skills	1. 2. 3.
Cognition	1. 2. 3.
Challenging behavior	1. 2. 3.

Assessment of Everyday Routines and Activities

Child's name: _____ Caregiver interviewed: _____ Date: _____

DIRECTIONS: List the child's everyday routines and activities, and indicate a rating from 1–4 for each.

1: The child enjoys the routine and is actively engaged with others.

2: The child is calm and content during the routine but not actively engaged with others.

3: The child engages in mildly challenging behaviors during the routine.

4: The child engages in severely challenging behaviors during the routine.

Circle the routines and activities that you would like to target for intervention.

Home		School		Community	

Ecological Assessment
for Everyday Routines

(page 1 of 2)

Child's name: _____ Routine: _____ Date: _____

Opening statement	Caregiver response and/or information gathered from direct observation
Describe what the routine looks like. (Consider how your child participates and the behaviors of others involved in the routine.)	

Probing questions	Caregiver response and/ or information gathered from direct observation	Possible next steps
Describe how your child communicates during the routine.		

*Bringing ABA to Home, School, and Play for Young Children
with Autism Spectrum Disorders and Other Disabilities by Debra Leach
Copyright © 2012 by Paul H. Brookes Publishing Co., Inc. All rights reserved.*

Probing questions	Caregiver response and/ or information gathered from direct observation	Possible next steps
Describe how your child socially interacts during the routine.		
Describe how your child participates independently during the routine.		
Describe cognitive skills your child demonstrates during the routine.		
Does your child engage in any challenging behaviors during the routine?		

ABA Activity-Based Instruction Matrix

Child's name: _____ Date: _____

DIRECTIONS:

1. List the domain-specific goals across the top of the table using an abbreviation for the goal or a number to represent the goal.
2. List the routines selected for ABA interventions down the left side of the table.
3. Put X's in the boxes to indicate which goals will be addressed during which routines. Instead of X's, the initials of the caregiver who will implement the intervention during the specific routine can be indicated if desired. This allows multiple caregivers to share responsibility for implementing the interventions.

	Goal:	Goal:	Goal:	Goal:	Goal:
Routine:					
Routine:					
Routine:					
Routine:					
Routine:					

Goals for Targeted Routine

Child's name: _____ Routine: _____ Date: _____

Domains	Goals
Communication skills	
Social interaction skills	
Independence	
Cognitive skills	
Positive behaviors	

ABA Teaching Plan Template

Child's name: _____ Domain: _____

Objective	Routines to target

Data collection procedures: _____

Explanation of data collection procedures:

Teaching procedures:

1.

2.

3.

4.

5.

Intervention Plan for Targeted Routine

Child's name: _____ Routine: _____

	Goals	Behavioral strategies
Communication		
Social interaction		
Independence		
Cognition		
Positive behaviors		

Percentage Correct Data Sheet

Child's name: _____

Goal: _____

TRIALS	Date:	Date:	Date:	Date:	Date:
10	C / I 100%	C / I 100%	C / I 100%	C / I 100%	C / I 100%
9	C / I 90%	C / I 90%	C / I 90%	C / I 90%	C / I 90%
8	C / I 80%	C / I 80%	C / I 80%	C / I 80%	C / I 80%
7	C / I 70%	C / I 70%	C / I 70%	C / I 70%	C / I 70%
6	C / I 60%	C / I 60%	C / I 60%	C / I 60%	C / I 60%
5	C / I 50%	C / I 50%	C / I 50%	C / I 50%	C / I 50%
4	C / I 40%	C / I 40%	C / I 40%	C / I 40%	C / I 40%
3	C / I 30%	C / I 30%	C / I 30%	C / I 30%	C / I 30%
2	C / I 20%	C / I 20%	C / I 20%	C / I 20%	C / I 20%
1	C / I 10%	C / I 10%	C / I 10%	C / I 10%	C / I 10%

Level of Independence Data Sheet

Child's name: _____

Goal	Date:	Date:	Date:	Date:	Date:	Date:	Date:	Date:
	4	4	4	4	4	4	4	4
	3	3	3	3	3	3	3	3
	2	2	2	2	2	2	2	2
	1	1	1	1	1	1	1	1
Goal	Date:	Date:	Date:	Date:	Date:	Date:	Date:	Date:
	4	4	4	4	4	4	4	4
	3	3	3	3	3	3	3	3
	2	2	2	2	2	2	2	2
	1	1	1	1	1	1	1	1
Goal	Date:	Date:	Date:	Date:	Date:	Date:	Date:	Date:
	4	4	4	4	4	4	4	4
	3	3	3	3	3	3	3	3
	2	2	2	2	2	2	2	2
	1	1	1	1	1	1	1	1

1 = Maximum prompting   2 = Moderate prompting   3 = Minimal prompting
4 = Independent

Frequency Data Sheet

Child's name: _____

Goal: _____

	Date	Date	Date	Date	Date	Date
Total _____	10	10	10	10	10	10
of _____	9	9	9	9	9	9
_____	8	8	8	8	8	8
_____	7	7	7	7	7	7
per _____	6	6	6	6	6	6
	5	5	5	5	5	5
	4	4	4	4	4	4
	3	3	3	3	3	3
	2	2	2	2	2	2
	1	1	1	1	1	1
	0	0	0	0	0	0

Yes/No Data Collection Sheet

Child's name: _____

Goal	Date	Date	Date	Date	Date	Date	Date	Date	Date
	Y N	Y N	Y N	Y N	Y N	Y N	Y N	Y N	Y N
	Y N	Y N	Y N	Y N	Y N	Y N	Y N	Y N	Y N
	Y N	Y N	Y N	Y N	Y N	Y N	Y N	Y N	Y N
	Y N	Y N	Y N	Y N	Y N	Y N	Y N	Y N	Y N

Index

Page references ending with *f* or *t* indicate figures or tables.